MW00564669

The
AGENT'S
EDGE

JORDAN COHEN
WITH MARK TABB

The
AGENT'S
EDGE

Secret Strategies
to Win Listings and
Make Your Fortune
Selling Real Estate

HarperCollins
LEADERSHIP

AN IMPRINT OF HARPERCOLLINS

© 2023 Jordan Cohen

All rights reserved. No portion of this book may be reproduced, stored in a retrieval system, or transmitted in any form or by any means—electronic, mechanical, photocopy, recording, scanning, or other—except for brief quotations in critical reviews or articles, without the prior written permission of the publisher.

Published by HarperCollins Leadership, an imprint of HarperCollins Focus LLC.

Any internet addresses, phone numbers, or company or product information printed in this book are offered as a resource and are not intended in any way to be or to imply an endorsement by HarperCollins Leadership, nor does HarperCollins Leadership vouch for the existence, content, or services of these sites, phone numbers, companies, or products beyond the life of this book.

Book design by Aubrey Khan, Neuwirth & Associates, Inc.

ISBN 978-1-4002-3765-4 (eBook)
ISBN 978-1-4002-3770-8 (HC)

Library of Congress Control Number: 2023931451

Printed in the United States of America
23 24 25 26 27 LBC 5 4 3 2 1

This book is lovingly dedicated to

my amazing wife, Rebecca,

my children, Cameron and Cassidy,

and my parents, Arnie and Harriet Cohen

CONTENTS

PART 2

BEYOND THE LISTING: SOME OTHER THINGS I'VE LEARNED

FOREWORD

by Sylvester Stallone

I've met many people in my lifetime, thousands upon thousands, a vast ocean of humanity! One of the downsides of being famous, and there really are not many, is you pretty much have seen it all and done it all, so needless to say it takes a minor explosion, a seismic event, an atomic bomb of a personality to get my attention . . .

Well, folks, one day that dynamo presented itself, and I can honestly say I've never met, or will ever meet, such a one-in-a-billion individual such as Jordan Cohen!

His enthusiastic energy could easily light up the entire state. His infectious personality is only matched by his unflagging ability to stand and deliver on his word! Which I found to be a bond he takes as a devout commitment—if he says he's going to accomplish the Task, you can go to sleep knowing he will be wide awake Accomplishing the Task!

Jordan is so damn good at his profession I can safely say there is no one better I've dealt with. I mean that, these words are coming from my heart, not my mind. A remarkable businessman, a devoted family man, loyal and appreciative of his clients; I can safely say I've never seen him without a smile so bright that it causes me to smile, whether I want to or not!

I simply love the guy, and it makes me very pleased to call this "memorable" man my permanent friend.

KEEP PUNCHING,
SYLVESTER STALLONE

AUTHOR'S NOTE

Before we get started, I want to say thank you for picking up my book. From the bottom of my heart, thank you. Never in my wildest dreams did I ever think I would be in this position when I started selling real estate thirty-plus years ago. Now that I am, I'm grateful and humbled by the thought that you would take the time to read what I have to say. This book truly was thirty-plus years in the making. It is my legacy, and I am fired up to share with you what I do and what has made me successful. I know these lessons will help you as well.

JORDAN COHEN

INTRODUCTION

Why Another Real Estate Book?

I landed my first listing the way most of us probably do: family. My girlfriend Becky's parents retired with a plan to move out of their San Fernando Valley tract home where they'd lived for forty years and into their dream home. Becky told them, "Jordan just got his real estate license. You should let him sell it for you." They did and I did, but not without making every rookie mistake in the book . . . and a few that I came up with all on my own. That was in 1991. Thirty years later in 2021, as an individual agent, I sold $314 million in residential properties in Southern California, making me the number one RE/MAX agent in the world. So how did I go from selling $100,000 tract homes to selling mansions worth tens of millions of dollars? I can't wait to tell you. By the way, I used that first commission check to buy an engagement ring, and Becky and I have been together ever since.

I titled this book *The Agent's Edge* for a reason. In the pages that follow, I share with you many of the processes, scripts, and strategies I've developed over the past three decades to become a successful listing agent. Whether you specialize in luxury properties or starter homes or something in between, these strategies have worked very well for me, and I believe they will work for you as well. But before we get started, I need you to know that this isn't a motivational book. I will not dazzle you with stories of how I prepare myself to succeed every day. I don't drink carrot juice. I don't exercise. I don't dress for success in fancy suits. I do not tell myself affirmation statements or make vision boards or any of the things you expect from a motivational speaker because I'm not a motivational speaker. I sell real estate as a solitary agent along with my two assistants.

While I am a salesman, this is not a book of general principles you can apply to any type of sales. I sell real estate. It's what I know, and I'm good at it. Over the past thirty-plus years, I've found a formula that works, and I wrote this book to share it with you. It's a proven formula, but it won't work with cars or insurance, only real estate.

Finally, let me assure you that I do not claim to have found *the* secret formula no one else has ever thought of for making a consistent living selling real estate. There are many real estate trainers out there, and they all have their own unique scripts, dialogues, and ideas that work. I have attended dozens of their seminars myself over the years and have taken bits and pieces from them all.

But I found my business groove only once I committed to do my own thing. And my own thing isn't that complicated. You'll probably slap your head at least a couple of times while reading this book and say, "Why didn't I think of that?" Believe me, I've had plenty of times where I wondered why I hadn't thought of some of these things earlier in my career. Real estate isn't rocket science. That's one of the reasons why it is such a hot career choice. You don't need an MBA or a PhD or even a college degree to get your license. You take a few weeks of classes, pass a multiple-choice exam, and you are on your way. That's what I did. But I quickly found I needed much more than a license to build a career.

As I write this at the beginning of 2022, there are more than twice as many real estate agents as there are properties for sale in the United States. We're all looking for an edge. That's all I offer you in these pages. An edge. If by the time you close the back cover you have discovered one or two tips that will make a difference in your career, this journey we are taking together will be worth it. (But I think you will find a lot more than one or two.)

I hope you find this book to be practical. Whether you are considering a career change into real estate, just starting out, or a seasoned pro, I have walked in your shoes. I can trace this book's roots to a day six months into my career when I lost out on my first two listing appointments. Those two houses would have made me $6,000 each. Back then $6,000 would have doubled my net worth and made it possible for me to move out of my parents' house. I made up my mind that day that I was going to prepare myself to win. And that's what success in real estate comes down to: winning in a competitive situation against friends and colleagues.

I didn't know what I needed to do to win when I first started. After I missed out on those two listings, I maxed out my credit cards going to every seminar and workshop I could find. I talked to every successful agent I could corner for a conversation, and I convinced a successful agent in my area to mentor me. I then took all I had learned and, through the process of trial and error, figured out what worked for me and what didn't. Then I practiced and practiced and practiced and practiced like my career depended on it—because it did. Before long I started winning listings and making sales. I even bought my own starter home and got out of my parents' house. Over the years I revised my strategies as I moved from starter homes to a nicer middle-class neighborhood and ultimately to the ultraluxury market where I've worked for the past twenty-plus years. The markets changed, but the basics of what works did not. I am convinced that if you can sell, you can sell anywhere. You just have to take advantage of every opportunity when they arise . . . and they will arise.

Again, I cannot tell you how grateful I am that you picked up this book. I love what I do, and it's given my family and me a very nice life. That's why when I was approached about writing a book I jumped at the chance. I figure if a guy like me, an ordinary guy from a middle-class family who squeaked by in school, can reach these levels of success, so can you.

1

STARTING OFF RIGHT?

Real estate is the only profession I know that gives you the opportunity for unlimited income while letting you choose your own hours. You don't have to start at the bottom and wait for a promotion to move up the ladder of success, and you do not need a college degree to do well. You can take your career as far as you want to go, and you can earn as much as you want to earn. No one sets limits on what you can accomplish except you! That's why I love what I do and why I wrote this book. For the new agent, my goal is to give you the playbook that I used to go further in this business than I ever dreamed possible. For those of you who have been at this for a while, I hope you will discover some tips and insights from my experience selling real estate at a very high level that can make you more productive. Whether real estate is your full-time job or a side hustle, all of us are always looking for an edge to lift us to that next level. I hope you find yours here.

Why I Chose Real Estate

Thanks in part to reality TV, real estate is a hot career choice. That wasn't true when I started out in 1990. Back before HGTV and *Million Dollar Listing* glamorized buying and selling homes, the stereotypical real estate agent was a middle-aged man or woman who had either burned out or washed out of another career and thought, *What the hell, I might as well try real estate.* Classes for the real estate license exam took all of two weeks, and even I passed the multiple-choice test on my first try. I guess what I am saying is, thirty-plus years ago, "real estate agent" was not exactly the gold standard when it came to career choices, although you saw a lot of gold jackets in the profession thanks to the marketing efforts of Century 21. But it appealed to those of us with an entrepreneurial spirit. Since every agent essentially works for themselves even though we work under a broker, becoming a real estate agent was like starting your own business without having to put any money down.

I was introduced to the business by my parents. For most of my youth my dad owned a hamburger stand and my mom was a manicurist. At some point in life they both decided they were sick of what they were doing and decided to give real estate a whirl. After passing their license exams and working for various real estate companies, they both eventually found a home at the Todd C. Olson brokerage in Northridge, California. The move worked out well for my parents both financially and emotionally. My dad seemed to enjoy selling houses a lot more than selling hamburgers.

The business was a lot different in the preinternet dark ages of the 1980s. Prospective home buyers could not go online and scroll through page after page of houses and click on photographs of every room. They couldn't even legally access the Multiple Listing Service (MLS) book. Buyers lived at the mercy of whatever homes an agent chose to show them.

The situation was just as bad for sellers. Marketing opportunities didn't go much beyond sticking a sign in front of a house or placing ads in local papers. The one exception came in the form of the *Los Angeles Times* and the *Daily News* weekly real estate sections of their San Fernando Valley editions. Both papers ran press releases on area homes for sale, complete with a photograph or two. The best part about them: both were free and had a wide reach. You just had to figure out a way to get your listings featured. Needless to say, competition for those few slots was fierce. A press release or two in the papers could make the difference between a good sales year and a bad one. Sellers always got happier when they saw their home in the paper, while those who didn't often wondered what their agent was doing to promote their houses.

My parents had tried to get homes in both papers without much success. By this point I was a student at Cal State, Northridge, studying communications and marketing. Like every other college student, I was always looking for a way to make money. When my mom offered me fifty dollars to go take pictures of one of her listings and write something to submit to the papers on the off chance they might run it, I jumped at the chance. Rather than take a couple of snapshots and write a generic listing description, I asked myself what I could do to make my mom's submission stand out. I went out and took some great photos of her listing. Rather than turn in a handwritten description of the house, I hired a friend to edit and type my submission to give it a professional look. When I took the release to the *L.A. Times*, I didn't just drop off the packet. I found the desk of the nice lady who decided what went in the paper and hand delivered it to her. I may have also turned on a little charm and played up the whole struggling college student angle. It worked, and it kept working every time I brought her a new submission.

I did so well for my parents that I decided to expand beyond their properties. I started a little business I called Property Promotions and offered my services to other real estate agents in the San Fernando Valley. Before long, I was making nearly a thousand dollars a week, which was great money for a college kid. I also befriended a cool guy named Manny who was the real estate section decision maker at the *Daily News*. At least once a month his favorite bottle of tequila just happened to come with my submissions. I'm not saying the tequila influenced his decision-making, but my properties almost always ended up in the paper. Through Property Promotions I got to know most of the agents in the San Fernando Valley. To be honest, meeting so many gave me second thoughts about pursuing real estate as a career after college. I met a few real estate rock stars, but the majority just got by. And I wanted to do more than get by.

A chance meeting completely changed my perspective. I dropped by a local brokerage called Paramount Properties one afternoon to pick up an assignment for Property Promotions. In the middle of my conversation with Syd, the broker, he pointed out an agent named Shawn. "See that guy over there," Syd said. "He's our best agent. He's going to pull down around four hundred grand this year." Keep in mind this was around 1989 or 1990. Four hundred thousand dollars was more than the average player in the National Football League made. And this guy was doing it selling houses! Real estate suddenly looked much more attractive to me.

I still wasn't completely sold on real estate after I graduated from Cal State, Northridge, with my rock-solid 2.05 GPA. Even though I was the first person in my family to graduate from college, my less than impressive grades didn't exactly have major corporations lining up to hire me. My little college business, Property Promotions, had done great . . . for a college kid. But nothing about it was unique enough to give it any kind of growth potential or long-term viability. I enjoyed sales and had always thought that's where I'd end up, but what to sell was the question. Eventually, I narrowed my choices down to real estate, because I was so familiar with it, and insurance, because I'd heard agents did pretty well for themselves. Going to my gym one day made my mind up for me.

I was on the bench press, doing my reps, when a guy came up to me. "Hey, I'm Jim," he said as he pulled a business card out of his sweat socks. "I'm the insurance guy. So how are you doing, insurance wise? Young guy like you, you probably haven't thought about life insurance yet, but it's not too early. You really should consider . . ." I looked around the gym and saw everyone in the gym scatter like roaches when the lights come on. I finished my reps while Jim kept talking and talking. After I dropped the weights, I made up an excuse about having to get to an appointment and got out of there as fast as I could. A short time later, I signed up to take the real estate exam classes. To this day I have never carried business cards.

Learning the Hard Way

After I passed my real estate license exam, I immediately started looking for the right brokerage to work for. I narrowed my choices down to two that happened to be right across the street from one another: Paramount Properties and Todd C. Olson, where my parents worked. Shawn worked out of Paramount Properties, and I knew I could learn a lot from him. Many of the agents in the office also broke the mold by being younger than the typical agent. Even though most of them were still ten years older than me, they were still at least ten years younger than every other agent in the Valley. During my interview with Syd, Paramount's owner, he offered me a job but then he added, "Since you are brand new and will need extra attention from me and our other agents, I'm going to start you out at a 60/40 split until you hit a million dollars in sales. After that I'll bump you up to the normal 80/20."

Syd wasn't insulting me. Starting off new agents with a 60/40 split, where 60 percent of my commission went to me and forty percent to the brokerage, was the industry standard for brand new agents. If anything, he was doing me a favor by even offering me a job, because this guy was and is a real estate genius. He'd hired Property Promotions many times to do press releases, which gave me a front row seat to see him and his office in action. If I had been smart, I would have jumped at his offer before he changed his mind. But I was young and cocky and had another option, so I thanked him for his time and told him I'd think about it.

I then went across the street to Todd C. Olson for whom I also had incredible respect. Todd was, and still is, the ultimate professional. At six feet, two inches tall, impeccably dressed in his crisp, white dress shirt and perfectly tied tie, with a dazzling gold Rolex on his left wrist, he almost seemed bigger than life. Any time Todd walks into a room, all eyes land on him. The man was, and is still today, a stud. Even before I went in for an interview, I looked at him as a role model, as a walking definition of what success looked like. I blame my lifelong obsession with Rolex watches on Todd. As soon as I was able, I bought a gold one, just like his, although I could only afford a used one at the time.

My interview went well. Todd also offered me a job, but instead of starting out with a 60/40 split, he offered to start me out at 80/20. I did the math in my head. Taking the job with Paramount was going to cost me $6,000 in lost commissions until I hit the magic million-dollar mark in sales. *Why would I give up six grand to go work at Paramount instead of Olson?* I asked myself. Here I was, a twenty-three-year-old kid fresh out of college with offers to work for two great offices. The way I saw it, I should go with the one that gave me the chance to make the most money from the start, which is why I took the job with Todd Olson.

Looking back thirty years later, I have no regrets for the decision I made. Todd was great to me the entire time I worked for him. But, if I were starting out today, I'd make finding a brokerage with a top-notch training program a higher priority than saving myself a few thousand dollars. Training then was not what it is now. Most of mine came in the form of advice older agents passed down to all the new guys. At the start, that advice felt like enough. My first buyer dropped into my lap one day at an electronics store. I don't even remember exactly what I went into the store to buy, but in the middle of the conversation with the salesclerk, he asked me what I did for a living. "I'm a real estate agent," I said.

"That's funny. I'm looking to buy a home," he replied. A few days later I took him to see several houses. He made an offer on one; the seller accepted it; and just like that I had my first buyer-side sale. *How easy was that?* I thought, and it was easy. That's the thing about real estate. You can make money fast if the stars line up just right, but it can take years to master the skills you need to be successful long term.

My first listing (as you learned in the introduction) also fell in my lap. Becky's parents had just retired and bought a nice new tract home for $90,000 in the Inland Empire community of Sun City in Southern California. Now they needed to sell their house of thirty years in Canoga Park. Becky told them I had my real estate license and had just landed my first job, to which they replied, "You think Jordan can sell our house?" "Of course," she told them, and just like that, I had a listing.

I thought I was ready . . . even though deep down I had no idea what I was doing. At least I acted like I was ready. I took Becky's parents through all the preliminary steps to get their house ready to put on the market. I did not have any kind of marketing plan, which will come as a surprise when you discover I devote six chapters of this book to how to sell oneself as an expert marketer during the listing presentation. The other agents in my office talked about how important an open house is, so I figured I should give one a try. Again, I had no skills. I did not know how to set up the open house or the best way to engage with potential buyers and distinguish between those who were serious from the neighbors who came along just to get a look inside. I had yet to learn that for many people, going to open houses and looking at homes is cheaper than going to a movie.

They say even a blind squirrel finds an acorn every once in a while, and that was me. A couple came to my open house, looked around a while, then asked, "What are you asking?" I told them, $219,000. They looked at each other for a moment and then said, "We'll take it," without trying to talk me down. What should have been a red flag only made me feel good about myself. Only the best agents got full asking price in that market, and I did that my first time negotiating a deal. I asked the couple how much they planned to put down, and they told me 10 percent. Although 20 percent is always preferable, I told them, no problem. I could make this work. After all, $22,000 was more money than I had ever seen, so I assumed their loan was guaranteed. I pulled out the one-page contract (DocuSign was science fiction back then) and told the buyers to sign here, press hard, and the third copy is yours.

Once the paperwork was signed and I closed down the open house, I called Becky's parents. I was walking on air. Not only did I get them their price, I had also sold their house fast. That had to make them feel a little better about their daughter's future with me. My enthusiasm did not dim when the lender told me the buyers' down payment actually came from one of their mothers, who had to refinance her home to come up with the money. I didn't care how they came up with the money, the important thing to me was we had a deal. And I was going to hit the lottery with more than $12,000 in commission.

With the house as good as sold, Becky's parents moved into their new home. Thirty days into escrow, the buyers called and asked, "Would it be possible for us to go ahead and move into the house before closing?" Without discussing the question with my broker, I told them I did not see how that would be a problem. After all, the house was empty, and it was going to be theirs in a couple of weeks. I called Becky's parents, who asked me what I thought. Like every buyer and seller, they depended on my expertise. "I don't see why not," I told them. The buyers then moved in, and I started thinking about taking my commission check straight to the jewelry store for a very important purchase.

My world came to a screeching halt three days before closing. The lender called me. "Jordan, we have a problem. Your buyers did not qualify for the mortgage."

"What?" I asked. "I didn't think that could happen, especially not this close to closing."

"As you must know, loan contingencies are open until the escrow closes," I was told. "We're sorry."

I hung up the phone and walked out of the office. I dropped down on the curb and sat with my head in my hands; I was nearly in tears. The rules have since changed, and this scenario could never happen today, but it did then, and I was blindsided. *How am I going to get out of this mess?* I asked myself over and over. I didn't have an answer. As far as I could see, I'd blown it. And then another thought hit me, which sent shivers down my spine: *What will the love of my life think about me?* which was quickly followed by, *How am I going to explain this to her parents?*

As I sat on the curb, Todd Olson came outside. "What's going on, Jordan?" he asked. I told him the whole, horrible story. "Why didn't you ask me for help from the start?" he asked. Now that was the magic question. Why *hadn't* I asked for help? There was really only one answer: I was too proud to ask. I thought I knew everything I needed to know, and what I didn't know I could figure out on the fly. Sitting on the curb, my world falling apart around me, I didn't have an ounce of pride left in me. I asked Todd for help, and we found another lender. In the end, we still closed on the house, albeit two weeks later than originally planned. Becky's parents weren't too happy with me, but they did not hold my screwup against me since they accepted me into the family when I asked their daughter to marry me. The half-carat, marquise-cut diamond engagement ring I bought with the commission check helped.

My Life-Changing Failure

So how did I go from making every mistake in the book in my first deal to becoming the number one RE/MAX agent in the world? I wish I could say I immediately learned from my mistakes and jumped on the fast track to success. Unfortunately, I still had a lot of mistakes to make before that could happen, beginning with my search for my next listing.

When I took the job with the Todd C. Olson brokerage, I did not know I had stepped into an agency filled with great geographical farmers. Of course, the only farming I had heard of involved putting seeds into dirt. The farmers in the agency explained how geographical farming means targeting a specific area with the goal of becoming a household name there. Then, when people in that area decide to put their home on the market, they are more likely to call on you. The more homes in the area where you farm, the better your chances of getting listings. "You should start where you've already had some success," I was told. Since I sold my first home in Canoga Park, that became my default geographical farm.

I wasn't quite sure how one sale in a neighborhood of over five hundred homes translated into name recognition for me, but I did what I was told. I started farming Canoga Park with every tool the other geographical farmer agents shared with me. I did cold callings. I sent out mailers. I knocked on doors. I did drop contests. I gave away pumpkins and Chip Clips and jar openers, all with my name printed on them in big letters. I don't think I would ever entrust the sale of my biggest asset to someone whose name I saw on the clip keeping my Cheetos fresh, but that's what we did back in the preinternet, pre–social media dark ages. I also maxed out my credit cards attending seminar after seminar and doing everything they taught me about prospecting. Months went by and I still wasn't getting anywhere.

But then a miracle happened, and the skies parted. I received not one but two invitations to come interview for listings back-to-back. Immediately, I did the math in my head. Each house was probably going to go for around $150,000, which meant my commission on the two (and I assumed I'd get both) was going to double my entire net worth. Better yet, it would get me out of my parents' house before my wedding date.

On the day of the interviews, I dressed for success in my best pair of half-polyester/half-wool Sansabelt slacks, with the elastic waistband, and my sharpest looking short-sleeved dress shirt along with a wide-angle tie my dad gave me. I also put on my fake gold watch to make the potential sellers think that I was a real player in this industry. I then drove over to each listing in my old used Honda Accord with aftermarket chrome rims, strode up to the door carrying my trusty briefcase, the same briefcase I received as a bar mitzvah gift in 1979, and knocked on the door. I think I had taken maybe two steps into the first house when it hit me: I spent all my time working to get these listing interviews but virtually no time preparing for the interview itself. I guess I figured I could wing it on the advice other agents gave me.

"Tour the house with the sellers and act like you love the house," I'd been told, so that's what I did. The first couple took me through each room and pointed out all the things they loved about their home. I nodded along and said things like, "Oh yeah, that looks great. I think buyers will really love this too," when I actually had no idea whether the six-inch baseboards the husband had installed himself even mattered. But I said they did because I wanted to make a good impression by telling the sellers exactly what they wanted to hear.

After the tour we went back to the living room. I sat down on the oversized floral couch opposite the couple, and they looked at me like, *Okay, now what?* Most of the seminars I attended stressed the importance of talking about price right up front. "If the seller has an unrealistic price in mind, it's best to cut off the interview and leave rather than waste your time for a listing you won't be able to sell," I had learned, so I started talking about the price of their home. I pulled out comps in the neighborhood and had the same conversation these sellers probably had with every other real estate agent they interviewed.

"Tell the seller about your brokerage and what it brings to the table," I was told, so after the price conversation ran out of steam, I started talking about the Todd C. Olson brokerage. Unfortunately, we were a small, local brokerage. While Todd C. Olson was a familiar name in the Valley, it didn't have the clout of a national brand like Century 21, RE/MAX, or Coldwell Banker. That part of the interview went rather quickly.

With nothing else to say, I then thanked the couple for their time and told them I hoped they chose to list with me.

They didn't. Neither did the other potential listing. Both went with more experienced agents. I felt like I had just run into a brick wall. Here I was, twenty-three years old, flat broke, living with my parents with no end in sight. I felt like a complete loser. *Man, this has got to change*, I told myself.

Over the next few days I stepped back and thought over how both rejections went down. I asked myself, *Why did they go with the other agents and not me?* The other agents had more experience, but there had to be more to it than that. That made me ask, *How can I change the equation so that I win way more often than I lose?* The answer to that question put me on the path that led to where I am today. It is also the heart of this book, beginning with the next chapter.

2

THE KEY TO SUCCESS

I'm a real estate agent in _____ and I'm having the hardest time succeeding. I left my corporate finance position to pursue real estate because I love it so much. I'm cold-calling so much but getting no response with an actual listing. All I want to be is a listing agent and, of course, work with serious buyers too. I've been an agent for a year and three months. Of course, I will continue and not give up, but I really hope one day I reach where you are today.

I am humbled that fellow real estate agents reach out to me like this almost every day. The writer speaks for many of us when she says, "All I want to be is a listing agent." Listing agents are always the top agents in every neighborhood, every town, every city, every state, every country around the globe. No exceptions. A strong listing inventory guarantees you make money. I realize I'm not telling you anything you don't already know. This is Real

ate 101. The more listings you have, the more consistent
ney you will make in any market, good or bad. Year in and
year out, listing agents are always the top agents. No ifs, ands, or
buts about it.

Now don't get me wrong. I love working with buyers and help-
ing them find the perfect house. Buyer sales are fantastic. They give
instant gratification and a quick infusion of cash. At least 25 percent of my business is buyer-represented transactions. I look at
every buyer closing as a gift, like an unexpected bonus. But I built
my business through listings, and they remain the backbone of
what I do today. That is why I believe *the* best way to excel in any
market and build a long-term, sustainable career, is to become a
listing agent.

But, and this is why I receive a message like the one above nearly
every day, let's get real: building a listing inventory is much easier
said than done. Almost all of us dream about becoming listing
agents, but for many of us, this dream always remains just out of
reach. It's not for lack of effort. When I first started out, I was
introduced to geographical farming by some of the best farmers
I've ever known. Even though my first attempt at farming didn't
turn out so well, I built my career with it. You can be the greatest
geographical farmer the world has ever seen, however, and still not
make it as a listing agent. You can also cold-call until you are blue
in the face and still not build a catalog of listings. Back in my early
days I made the bulk of my living by cold-calling expired listings,
but all the calls in the world alone do not automatically translate
into listings. Nor does sending out mailers. Or buying Zillow ads.
Or joining an incredible team that hand delivers leads to you. You
don't become a listing agent by plastering your face on bus benches,
supermarket conveyor belt food dividers, or the outfield fence at
the local high school baseball field. You can have a half million
followers on your Instagram account and millions of views on

YouTube, but followers and views don't guarantee anything except name recognition. All of these methods may open doors and get you a seat at a breakfast table across from potential sellers, but to win listings, you have to win that interview. And to win the interview, you must be prepared to knock it out of the park.

Now I understand that a lot of you reading this book win listings in your market and you've never given much thought to your listing presentation. After all, most agents have been trained to talk about the exact same things when we sit down with Mr. and Mrs. Seller: price, internet exposure on real estate sites, commissions, our experience, our companies, and our teams. We're programmed to believe sellers automatically choose the agent with whom they feel the most comfortable, so we try to come across as trustworthy. We have also been taught to develop a large network of contacts through coaching our kids' sports teams or attending places of worship or joining the Rotary or all the other ways we make ourselves visible in our communities to land listings. In the end, old-school training says winning a listing comes down to a seller deciding: "Hey, Jim's a good guy. After all, he's married to my sister. I think we should list with him." That's just how real estate has been done since Fred and Wilma put their cave on the market and moved next door to the Rubbles.

Here's the problem with conventional thinking: if we do what everyone else does, we end up asking the same question that my Instagram follower asked at the top of this chapter. "I'm doing everything I'm supposed to do, but nothing is getting me any closer to my goal of being a listing agent like you," she basically said. I understand exactly where she's coming from. Believe me. If I had kept trudging along doing the same old thing every other agent does after losing out on the two listings I wrote about in the last chapter, I'd probably be pulling business cards out of my sweat socks at the gym trying to sell insurance right now.

That's why I stepped back from losing two consecutive competitive listing interviews and told myself there had to be a better way. Ultimately, I realized that if becoming a listing agent is the best way to make a consistent living in real estate, why would I leave anything to chance? Why max out my credit cards and invest all my time and energy into marketing and prospecting to get a listing interview, only to go in and hope sellers prefer my way of saying the same thing they hear from every other agent they've interviewed?

My whole approach changed when I came to understand that winning listings is like winning any other competition. My hometown Los Angeles Rams did not win Super Bowl LVI by winging it. They might have won their championship on February 13, 2022, but the roots of that victory went back months before the season even started. The previous Super Bowl was hardly over when management started working on a strategy they hoped could lead them to the title. They made trades and signed players and hired coaches, all to put the pieces in place to carry out their strategy. In the weeks leading up to their first game of the season, they studied the competition. They scripted plays. They planned and they prepared, and they practiced until they had a championship-level game plan with championship-level players like three-time defensive player of the year Aaron Donald. He is addicted to the process of becoming the best. The hard work. The practice. The study of his opponents. All of it. Whatever it takes to be the best.

Real estate is no different.

To be great, we too have to be addicted to the process of becoming great. And that process all comes down to a great listing presentation because:

A great listing interview presentation is the key to success in real estate. Period!

We may sell starter homes or high-end luxury properties or something in between, but the same truth holds: a great listing presentation wins listing interviews and opens the door to consistent income and career longevity.

I started out selling tract homes in one part of the San Fernando Valley, then I moved on to intermediate homes in Northridge (home of the 1994 earthquake, and yes, I was there then), and today I sell luxury properties in Westlake Village and throughout all of Southern California. But here's the thing: my game plan has not changed. Everything I do builds on the foundation of my listing presentation. The presentation itself has evolved over the years, but the heart of it remains the same.

More Than a Script

Early in my career I attended a real estate seminar where a panel of some of the leading agents and trainers of the day took questions from the audience. Someone asked how the panelists responded when asked to discount their commission. The main trainer leaned forward, smiled, and said in a direct tone, "I tell them, 'No. Next question.'" The audience cheered like he'd just hit the winning home run in the bottom of the ninth for the home team, but I sat there and put myself in the position of a homeowner who might ask that question. If I'm interviewing agents to list my home, and one of them told me, "No. Next question," I'd think they were an arrogant SOB. I don't think most people want to hire an arrogant SOB to sell their home.

People will forget most of what we say before we are out of their driveway, (except for a line like "No. Next question"), but they remember how we say it. Arrogance turns them off, and so does uncertainty. If we stammer after a question like we don't know what we are doing, sellers pick up on that. They also cue into awkward pauses and "uhs" and "ohs" and every other sign we do not completely buy into what we are saying. If our presentation sounds forced or rehearsed, people will feel our insincerity. And sincerity matters. It may matter more than anything else we have to say because houses are not commodities. They are people's homes, which gives sellers a strong emotional connection to them. Often the decision to sell is about more than dollars and square footage and open-concept floor plans. Moving away from a home means packing up and leaving years, sometimes decades, of memories in the rearview mirror.

That is why my interview presentation is more than a script to be memorized. I obviously have language and a defined marketing plan I organize well in advance, language I will share with you for you to customize and make your own, but for me, my presentation comes down to connecting with the seller with confidence and sincerity. We may sell real estate, but we are first and foremost in the people business.

When I started working on my presentation, I studied everything I could find. I went to Daniel Penley seminars and Robert Evans seminars and Mike Ferry workshops. I attended them all. During the breaks I approached successful agents and peppered them with questions about how to respond to sellers' objections and questions. I talked to my own broker and all the agents in my office, seeking their input. Once I had exhausted all in-house authorities, I walked across the street from the brokerage where I worked over to Paramount Properties to find Shawn, the agent who had inspired me when I was trying to decide which career path to pursue. Over the next few months, I took him to lunch many times and asked him question after question. He also allowed me to sit in his office and listen as he cold-called expired listings. I was a sponge, and I wanted to soak up everything I could from someone successful.

While soaking up all the information I could get from every successful agent who would talk to me, I started practicing my own listing presentation. For six months I did not watch television. Becky played the role of the seller and I tried to talk her into letting me list her home. It was a good thing she'd already agreed to marry me because I don't know many women who would have agreed to spend every date listening to me trying to convince her to list her make-believe home with me. Becky threw every possible objection that I could think of at me, along with many she came up with on her own. If a potential seller might ask it, I wanted to be prepared to answer. I kept working and working until I answered the most common objections before they were even asked. I practiced how I walked up to a house and how I knocked on the door and the questions I asked during a home tour. I practiced and I practiced until I did not sound rehearsed. And then I practiced some more until I was ready to deliver my presentation with confidence and relatability.

And then it was game time. Armed with my new listing presentation, I started winning listing interviews far more often than I lost. My dream of becoming a listing agent slowly came together. Along the way I discovered a strong listing presentation did more than just win listing interviews. It completely transformed how I looked at myself, my work, and the way I conducted business. Most importantly: it made real estate fun. Here's how:

1. A strong listing presentation gives you confidence in yourself.

Whenever I see a listing go up in my geographical farm with another agent, I shake my head and say, *They should have interviewed me.* So much for not sounding like an arrogant SOB, right? Believe me when I say that is not my intent. I have nothing but respect for my fellow agents. Many are my closest friends. Real estate is an unbelievably competitive field, which I know from experience. Every day I go up against some of the very best in the business. I am not saying I am better than everyone else. I am just so passionate about what I do, and I know what I bring to the table, that I want every seller to at least interview me. This isn't arrogance. It's confidence. That's why all of my advertisements say, "Serious about selling? Interview Jordan Cohen . . . You'll be glad you did."

We all *have* to believe the same about ourselves. At the end of the day we must have the confidence in ourselves and our marketing plans that we *do* give the seller the best chance to sell their home for the most amount of money and the very best terms. Once you believe you bring a unique set of skills as a marketer and salesperson into every listing interview, you can deliver your presentation with confidence and enthusiasm. And enthusiasm is contagious.

2. A strong presentation makes the seller as confident in you as you are in yourself.

Winning the listing interview means far more than adding another house to your listing inventory. My goal in every interview is for the seller to believe in me and the expertise I bring to the table. Once I get to the end of my presentation, I want the seller not only to *want* to list with me, I want them to feel like they *need* to list with me. And that's what a strong presentation does. It instills confidence in the seller. I do this by anticipating most of the objections we all face and addressing them one by one before the questions can be asked. I also lay out in great detail exactly what I will do to maximize the exposure of their home to as many people as possible. Every seller who interviews me hears me say, "I only get paid when I sell your house, not when I list it. Some agents celebrate listings. I never do. If you list with me, that just means it's time for me to roll up my sleeves and get to work."

I also never tell sellers that I am excited to work *with* them to sell their home. Instead I say, "When you list with me, you are hiring me to work *for* you in the business of selling your house. I am fired up to go to work for you. Thank you for the opportunity." I say this to every single seller who lists with me because I am grateful that they would entrust me with selling their most valuable asset. I am not doing them a favor by gracing them with my skills. The listing interview is a job interview, and that's how we must approach it. Listen, in this business we have to put all ego aside. Winning the sellers' confidence goes beyond them seeing us as a great agent. Real confidence comes when they see us as a great agent who is all-in on the business of selling *their* home *for* them.

Never assume a potential seller already has this level of confidence in you just because you have a strong track record. This is especially true when someone calls and says they're not planning to interview any other agents. "We want you," they may say, the classic "come list me." I still insist on giving these sellers my full presentation. Why? I want the sellers to hear exactly what I will do for them. It is imperative for every seller to understand how hard we work and the skill set we have developed to become great salespeople. They need to know all about the marketing dollars we invest, along with the time and passion necessary to sell a home for top dollar. The more they respect us as professionals, the more influence we have throughout the entire process, from listing to sale to close.

3. A strong listing presentation gives you the confidence to recognize and take advantage of every opportunity.

Opportunity knocks every single day. When we have complete confidence in our listing presentations, we hear it when others don't.

Opportunity knocks at open houses. If you've done one, you've heard it. A couple comes in to take a look around, and at some point we should all ask, "Are you planning on selling your current home before you buy?" You'll get one of three answers: yes, no, or maybe. No usually means I plan to find the right house first, and then I'll sell. Whatever the answer, we always follow up with, "Do you already have an agent you're working with?"

More than half the time, people will reply, "We kind of promised my friend Jill whom we've known forever that we'd list with her." Everyone has a friend or a brother-in-law or a next-door neighbor who sells real estate. With nearly two million agents in the United States, it's hard *not* to know someone in the business.

The old standard next line is, "That's great. Well, if anything changes, I hope you will consider me." And that's the end of it . . . but not if we have a great listing presentation.

A potential seller having a friend in the business does not equal a closed door. Instead I gently push by asking, "I appreciate your loyalty to your friend. But if you thought I could do a better job of maximizing the exposure of your home and sell it for more money, would you still be committed to your friend?"

"Committed" is the key word. I've found most people are only committed to their spouses or partners. More often than not they ask me, "What exactly do you do differently?" That question is the sound of opportunity knocking.

"What do I do differently?" I reply with enthusiasm. "Just let me tell you a couple of things I do differently." I then go into a very abbreviated version of my listing presentation. I give them a slight taste of what I have to offer, and then I say, "I'd love to sit down with you and give you my entire marketing plan. After all, the job of a real estate agent is to maximize the exposure of your home to sell it. The more people that become aware of your home, the better the chance of getting someone to pay your price or more." The phrase "your price or more" always resonates with people. How many times have you heard someone say, "I'm only going to sell if

I get *my* price"? I hear it all the time, which is why I use this language and throw it back at them. Early in my career I used the phrase "fair market value." Experience has taught me most people do not want fair market value. They want more, which is why there are tens of thousands of overpriced listings in America right now. If these potential sellers are in the group of people who insist on more than fair market value, I am at least opening the door for that opportunity.

I then finish by saying, "Could you give me a half hour to interview for the job of selling your home? No obligation, of course, but even if you do not list with me, perhaps I can give you some new, fresh, and aggressive marketing strategies that your agent can use." All of this language comes directly from my listing presentation. In other words, I am passionately selling myself to get that listing interview.

4. A strong listing presentation wins listings, which leads to more listings.

Back when I worked primarily in the San Fernando Valley, I landed a good portion of my listing interviews through cold-calling expired listings. Anyone who has ever called an expired listing knows the seller usually isn't that thrilled to hear from you. The moment a listing expires, agents descend like vultures on a carcass, and no one wants to be that carcass.

One day I called an elderly woman whose listing had just expired. She'd already talked to all the vultures she ever wanted to talk to. From the moment she answered my call, she started taking out all her frustrations on me. "I don't want to talk to any more real estate agents!" she yelled. "All of you keep calling and I don't know why. I had my home on the market for a whole year, and it didn't sell. What makes all of you think you can magically do what my other agent couldn't?"

I took her question as a challenge. Using language from my listing presentation, I shared a few ideas I had for marketing her home. She still didn't want to listen. "I've heard everything," she grumbled. "You all do the exact same things." I did not give up. I mentioned a local television show on which I advertised my listings, something few other agents did at the time. Apparently, she had seen the show because her wall started to crack. "Okay," she said, "If you can get here in fifteen minutes, I'll talk to you." Then she added, "By the way, you know you're the one hundredth real estate agent who has called me today."

"One hundred is my lucky number," I said. "I'll be there in fifteen minutes. I think you'll be glad you gave me this chance."

"We'll see," she replied.

Fourteen minutes later I pulled up to her home in Reseda and gave her my listing presentation. I wasn't nervous. I wasn't put off by her attitude that made me think she was mad at the world. I knew I could help her with her home, and now I had my chance to show her.

Long story short, I got the listing and sold her home, something she had thought impossible. After we had accepted an offer, she told me, "Boy, Jordan, you sure did a good job. You know, my son is looking at selling his home. Do you only work here in the Valley?"

"No, I work in all areas. Where does your son live?"

"Calabasas. Do you work there?"

Calabasas is a high-end market, and I was a few years away from focusing on luxury homes exclusively. But I firmly believe that if you are a good real estate agent, your skill set will work anywhere. I wasn't going to let this opportunity slip away. "Absolutely," I replied.

She said, "You will like my son and his wife. They are great people. He's a producer on one of the top comedies on television right now. Have you ever heard of . . ." and she told me the name of the show. Of course I had heard of it. My family watched it every Friday night. I knew right then this had the potential to be a huge sale.

I interviewed with the woman's son, won the listing, and not only sold his home for a great price, but I also found him the home he later bought. All of this came about because I had a great listing presentation that I also used in my cold call. If not for my confidence in my presentation, I would have taken no for an answer from the woman and gone on to my next call. And I would have never interviewed for a listing in a market that was far above the places I normally worked. I'm sure we all have wonderful stories like this, and good agents have hundreds of these stories, but it all comes down to interviewing and winning.

That is the power of a great listing presentation, which a great agent will back up with action. It opens doors. It wins listings. It has the power to make the illusive dream of becoming a listing agent a reality.

So give me the presentation! you have to be thinking. I'm ready. Let's dive in!

PART 1

THE LISTING PRESENTATION

3

WHY SHOULD A SELLER LISTEN TO YOU?

Sellers care about two things: selling their home for the most money and getting the best possible terms. Period. They might say they want to find a buyer who will love their house as much as they do, but when the offers come in, 99.99 percent of the time they will choose the highest and best. That's not just human nature; that's business. A home is the largest investment most people will ever make. When it comes time to sell, they want to maximize that investment, not give it away. That means, when a seller starts interviewing real estate agents, they will choose the person they believe will deliver the highest and best. Our challenge is to convince them that we are that agent. And that process begins the moment they say yes to a listing interview.

Before the Interview

Most real estate trainers recommend asking a series of prequalification questions as soon as a potential client agrees to meet with you. Again, this is Real Estate 101. We all need to learn as much as we can about a seller before we show up at their door. The more questions we ask, the more we discover the seller's true motivation and whether it is even worth our time to go on the listing interview. Also, if we ask the right questions, we might land not only a listing but also a potential buyer to whom we can sell their next home.

My approach is a little different. When someone calls and asks about me listing their home, or if I find them through a cold call or some other prospecting method, I respond,

> "I sure do appreciate your call. I work so hard to get calls like this and I am grateful you thought of me. I am very excited for the opportunity to interview for the job."

And I mean it. Even though I have a very strong track record, I put all ego aside to let this potential client know that I do not take their call for granted. I also want to let them know from the start that I am genuinely excited about the prospect of working for them. Not *with* them, but *for* them, which we will talk about in much greater detail later. Why say all this? Sellers do not care as much about what we have done in the past as much as they care about what we are going to do for them now. Humble gratitude from the beginning lets them know that theirs is not just another listing in my inventory but a top priority for me.

I then ask,

> "If you don't mind me asking, where do you plan on moving?"

Then I shut up and listen. The seller may be looking to downsize or upgrade. In California, many sell to move to a state with lower taxes. In a hot market, some sellers want to cash out their equity then rent until prices come down. In a cold market, they want to sell before they lose more equity, rent for a while, then buy once prices bottom out.

Whatever their reason for selling, I tell them,

"Got it. Thanks for sharing."

The purpose behind asking where they plan to go next is to give us information we can later use in the listing presentation. After inquiring where they plan to move next, I ask,

"What day and time works best for you?"

Whenever possible, I want to be the first agent interviewed. I was not trained this way. Experienced agents and speakers at seminars drilled into my head the idea that you should always try to go last. I was even given scripts and dialogue to memorize to convince them to let me go last so that I could be the freshest voice in the sellers' heads when decision time arrived. But back in the days when I tried to be the last agent interviewed, I found myself frustrated time and again when I received a call that went, "Hey, Jordan. We know we were supposed to meet with you, but we just interviewed another agency, and we really like them and we have decided to list with them." I am a very competitive person. I hate to lose, and nothing stings more than losing a game where I never even got to step up to bat. That's why I try to be the first agent interviewed. I want to be the one who so impresses the seller that they cancel the rest of their interviews and list with me.

I know there are those who say that going first risks being forgotten by the time sellers have finished conducting all their interviews. To me, that's all the more reason to deliver an unbeatable presentation a seller simply cannot forget. Our goal should be to go in and raise the bar so high that whoever comes next cannot compete. Again, putting their home on the market is the biggest business decision most sellers ever make. I do not believe they will choose the last person they interview simply because they are tired of interviewing agents. They will choose the one who stands out in terms of professionalism, marketing plans, strategies, enthusiasm, distinct sales skills, and especially the perceived ability to get the seller's price or more.

The Tour

My approach when I first arrive at a home for an interview varies depending on how much time the sellers have permitted me or what my schedule dictates on that particular day. Normally, the first thing I do when I arrive, after telling them again how excited I am for the opportunity, is to say,

> "Thanks again for having me come over. I am looking forward to taking a tour."

Tours can be tricky because we do not want to spend all of our limited interview time looking at every single feature in every single room. Sellers do not always understand that. They may well believe the purpose of the tour is for us to see *everything* right then. That time will come after we get the listing. At this stage of the interview, however, I believe the most important part of the tour is getting to know the sellers. This is my chance to listen to them and discover what elements and amenities are most important about their home to them. To do that, I must listen, listen, and listen some more. I listen with a smile when the seller points out the ceiling fans that took several months to pick out, and I tell them how nice they are. I listen and nod my approval when the seller talks about the extra storage in his garage. I always say, "That is fantastic. People will love that." I listen so that I can come back to these features when I talk about how I plan to present their home to qualified buyers.

Again, I do this with very little commentary. All of us who have been in this business for a minute have seen some "interesting" features you know will make the home harder to sell. We've all walked into a room with wallpaper so outlandish that we freeze in our tracks, but the seller loves this wallpaper. They don't just love it; they have a strong emotional connection to it. If we point out how anyone buying this house will rip that wallpaper out before they move in, we immediately offend the seller, and any chance we had of getting the listing flies right out the window. At some point we may need to initiate conversation about the wallpaper, but the day of the interview is absolutely not the time for it.

Most people I encounter who love their home, also love to talk about it. Tours can easily drag on and eat up most of the time we've allotted for the interview. When I can tell the tour is going to take too long, I say,

"Mr. Seller, I appreciate you showing me your home. You may have noticed I am not taking thorough notes of all the elaborate details you have pointed out because, if you hire me, I will come back with my assistant, and we will spend as much time as necessary to get to know your home and its features as well as you do. A great salesperson must know the product they are selling inside and out."

Usually, most sellers will reply, "Oh, that's great. Then I guess we can move through this pretty quickly." That's the response I am looking for. I find most sellers appreciate our being respectful of their time. Please know: I care about their homes. It is their *home*, but once again I need to make sure I have enough time to deliver a winning presentation.

First Things First

Once the tour is over, it's time to sit down with the sellers and make our pitch. If you are like me, you were trained to talk about the price of the house right out of the gate. I did that for a while early in my career but not anymore. In my presentation, pricing is the last conversation we have, not the first. Now, I understand the logic behind leading with price. If the seller has an unrealistic expectation as to what their house can bring, it does not make sense to spend an hour or more on marketing. Time is money, and your time is better spent interviewing with sellers who have a reasonable chance of selling their home rather than wasting your time with a couple who believe their home is worth 25 percent more than realistic value. And we've all encountered these couples.

Here's what changed my mind about leading with price. Back when I led off my presentation by talking about price and I encountered sellers who had an overly inflated view of their home's worth, I did as I was trained. I thanked them for their time and ended the interview right then. Why waste time and money on an overpriced listing, right? But here was the problem. A few weeks after I skedaddled away from these illogical sellers, I saw their homes come on the market at a reasonable price. Every time this happened, I stared at the MLS and thought, *This could have been my listing!* And I needed all the listings I could get.

I asked myself: Why did the seller listen to another agent about correctly pricing their home and not to me? That led to my next question: Why should they listen to me? What had I done in our few minutes together to sell them on my "expertise" on pricing? Many sellers come into the listing interview suspicious. They're just waiting for us to give them a lowball number that will ensure a quick sale. The phrase "I'm not going to just give my house away" is already on the tip of their tongues before we say a word about pricing. Comps aren't enough to make them listen because we all come in with comps. Besides, most homeowners in America are convinced their home is worth more than the other homes in their area.

Bringing up pricing and comps in the beginning often puts the seller on the defensive right from the start. We don't want them on the defensive. We need the seller to trust us, which is why I decided I would rather begin with establishing my credibility with the seller. Once I establish credibility by showing sellers the investments I plan to make to sell their home, they might be more likely to listen to me about how to price their home. These other sellers had obviously listened to someone. I asked myself what I needed to do to earn that right, and that's when I moved the pricing discussion to the end of my presentation. I have a lot more to say about this, an entire chapter's worth of material, but that will come later when we get to that part of my listing presentation.

Putting Our Best Foot Forward

Instead of leading off by talking about price, my presentation begins:

"Ms. Seller, first of all, thank you again for the opportunity to interview for the job of selling your home. And that's exactly what this is for me, a job interview. This is my potential opportunity to work for you."

Many times people give me a look that tells me that this is a new way of thinking for them, and they like it. They like the idea of hiring someone and being the boss. Again, that's just human nature. For me, using these terms immediately lays my ego aside. It is my way of letting the seller know that I am aware and accept that they are in charge. I then continue:

"Now I am going to assume that you've either interviewed for a job yourself or interviewed others, right?"

I say this with a little smile and a nod of my head. The seller always says yes.

"Then you can appreciate the fact that I have a short window of time to put my very best foot forward."

Again, I nod as I say this to get them focused on what I am about to say.

"So I want to explain everything I plan to do for you from start to finish in order to maximize the exposure of your home. After all, the job of a real estate agent is to make as many qualified buyers as possible aware of your home, get them excited about it, show it to them with passion, and then get them to make a commitment to buy your home at your price or more."

I used two phrases that make the sellers' ears perk up: "qualified buyers" and "your price or more." Remember, sellers may say they are committed to their friend from work who sells real estate on the side, but when push comes to shove they will hire the agent they believe will sell their home for the most money and with the best terms possible. I tap into this desire by mentioning "qualified buyers" and "your price or more." I will go into much more detail about each in the next few chapters.

I then say in a humble tone,

"I know you are probably interviewing other brokers, which is a great idea. What I would like to do before I present my marketing plan, if it is okay with you, is to tell you a little about myself and my experience in order to establish some credibility."

Then I add with a nod of my head,

"Would that be okay?"

The seller always nods yes.

Like any other job interview, this is the part where I show the seller I am qualified for the job. When I was a young agent with limited experience, I knew I could not match up with the veterans. If I talked about my experience, all I could say was "I've sold one house for my future in-laws, and I nearly blew that deal by letting the buyers move in before they'd even qualified for their loan, and their loan ended up getting turned down." Perhaps I could have gotten away with exaggerating my track record back in 1991, but there's no way inflating my success will work today when sellers have the ability to google us before we step into their home. So here's what I came up with.

For the new agents out there without a strong track record to build on, here's what I would say, and I would say it with confidence.

"Some of the agents you interview may have been at this for ten, twenty, even thirty years. I have not. And that's a great thing and here's why: I have been trained in today's market with today's techniques. I understand the current market and what it takes to make your home stand out. What worked twenty or thirty years ago may not work today, and that's why you need the skill set I bring to the table. I know how to maximize the internet and social media to get buyers as excited about your home as I am. I also have a team of seasoned professionals supporting me. I have phenomenal mentors, as well as a productive office and a support structure that backs me up and will make sure that everything that goes into selling your home, from the listing to showings to closing, will be a great experience for you."

In other words, when you cannot compete with other agents in terms of experience or sales production, compete in the area of expertise, confidence, and excitement. When I made that switch thirty years ago, I went from stammering my way through an interview to walking in with self-assurance.

Today, obviously, I am able to highlight my accomplishments. But you do not have to be the number one agent in the world or in your state or even your city to establish credibility with accomplishments of your own. Everyone wants to work with success. We'd all rather have a successful surgeon operate on us than one who has faced multiple malpractice lawsuits. If the IRS calls us in for an audit, we'd all rather have a successful accountant next to us. And when it comes time to sell a house, most people want to work with a successful agent.

So tout your success. If you were the top producer in your office last month, talk about it. If you sold four houses recently, emphasize it. If you have received any kind of award or special recognition, talk about it. If you sold 10, 15, or 20 percent more than the average real estate agent last year, use that. If sales haven't been so great lately, use testimonials from the past from very satisfied clients. If you work for a great company, talk about the company. To establish credibility, you want to show how you know what you're doing and that the seller can entrust the sale of their home to you.

The Payoff Pitch

This part of my presentation all leads up to one key statement I make to every single seller. I say,

> "Mr. Seller, I've told you a little of what I've done in the past, and I'm proud of what I've accomplished. I'm proud of the fact that I am the number one RE/MAX agent in the world out of 140,000 agents, but don't hire me because of that. Hopefully, you will hire me because of what I am going to do for you."

In other words:

- Don't hire me because I am the number one agent in Ventura County last year. Hire me because of what I am going to do for you now.

- Don't hire me because I know the best and latest real estate sales techniques, hire me because of how I am going to put those techniques to work for you.

- Don't hire me because I sold four other homes in your area over the past six months, hire me because of what I am going to do for you today.

- Don't hire me because my last ten clients all gave me five-star reviews, hire me because I am going to do everything I can to earn a five-star review from you as well.

I hope you will hire me because of what I can do for you. For the seller, that's the bottom line anyway. Our knowledge and experience and past sales and awards and accolades assure the seller that we know what we are doing. But what they really care about is what we are going to do *for them.* That's it! Yes, they want an agent who is up on the latest trends and techniques. Of course they want an agent with a track record of proven success. They want all of that, but at the end of the day, the one thing they care most about is what you are going to do *for them.*

I then add,

"I only get paid when I sell your home, not when I list it, which is why, if you hire me for this job, no one is going to work harder than me to get the job done and sell it for your price or better. The better I do my job, the more likely you will refer me to your friends and neighbors. I get it. I understand the importance of each and every deal. Now let me tell you how I plan to do that."

This is the payoff pitch and the perfect transition into the second part of the presentation: my marketing plan to maximize the exposure of their house to as many qualified buyers as possible.

Two Final Words

Before we move on to marketing, I need to make a couple of things clear. First, establishing credibility with sellers is crucial. We must be careful not to turn this part of the presentation into a bragging session, even though that's exactly what we are doing. We have to walk the fine line between establishing credibility and sounding like egomaniacs with inflated views of our own importance. Remember, we are not brain surgeons with decades of schooling and training. Nor are we schoolteachers who mold young minds. We took a two- or four-week class and passed a test to get our license. We aren't splitting the atom or ending world hunger. I sell houses along with nearly two million other people doing the exact same thing either full time or part time in the United States.

Now don't get me wrong. I love our profession. As I said in the first chapter, I think it is one of the best career choices you can make with its unlimited ceiling for earnings and advancement. We also provide an essential service that people truly need. But if we ever slip into the mindset that we have the most important job in the world or that the economies of the free world would collapse without us, then we have a serious problem. And sellers will see right through us.

I've found there are two ways to avoid this trap. First, be humble. Tonality is incredibly important here. How we speak as we list our accomplishments is just as important as what we say. Second, be brief. Sellers do not want to hear about everything you've ever done in your life. After I sell a home, I ask the sellers why they chose me as their listing agent as well as how I might improve my presentation. The biggest complaint I hear about other agents in their listing interviews is that they only talked about themselves. (The second complaint is that they only talked about comps; something we will talk about in the chapter on pricing.) I never want to be that guy who drones on and on about himself. Sellers care a lot more about what we are going to do *for them* than they do about what we have done in the past. That's what they want to hear, and we need to move quickly to it.

I also need to make it clear that your credibility in the eyes of the seller needs to go beyond the company for which you work. After I passed my real estate exam, I went to work for a small, independent brokerage, Todd C. Olson. At the time, we were not associated with a large, national real estate brand running commercials during ball games. Agents I went up against made a big deal about their companies. They told potential clients all about the size and reach of their national brands. I could not compete with that. Todd C. Olson was a local agency that was a major player in the San Fernando Valley, but no one outside of that area had ever heard of us. But after thinking through the problem, I found a way to level the playing field. Actually, I didn't have to level it. The field was as level as a pool table already, and it still is today. I simply needed to make the seller understand this.

Here's the language I came up with when I worked for a small brokerage. I asked the seller,

"Are you aware of the fact that as real estate agents, we are independent contractors? In other words, productive agents like me are like unrestricted free agents who can work in whichever office or company we want. In fact, we are constantly recruited to change brokerages. Let me tell you why I *chose* the Todd C. Olson brokerage. They let me do whatever I think is necessary to aggressively market your home. I don't have a ceiling over my head or broker-restricted rules! The brokerage and I have the same goals. I believe working for one of the giant corporations could actually limit my ability to market your home because they enforce too many restrictions and guidelines. As I mentioned before, I only get paid when I sell your home, not when I list it. So I have found Todd C. Olson gives me the freedom to market your home as aggressively as I wish."

With this I have turned the conversation around and made it appear that working for a small brokerage now gives me an advantage over those who lean on their national company's name to establish credibility. Obviously today I no longer work for a small, local brokerage. I'm part of the RE/MAX family, one of the largest and most recognized real estate companies in the world, and I love it. Thankfully, in RE/MAX, I work with a company that shares my goals and places zero limitations on me. That's part of why I chose RE/MAX. I enjoy not only the independence I am allowed under the umbrella of a global company but also the leadership and support from the top of the corporate ladder. Most importantly, I'm encouraged to promote my listings and my personal brand above all else.

Today I also add a very important fact. I tell sellers,

"You know, a company like RE/MAX is a fantastic company with a tremendous network of highly productive global agents. It's the most recognized real estate company in the world. But let's be real. Mr. Max isn't going to be the one showing your home or negotiating with buyers on your behalf. That is my job. Mr. Max is not going to curate just the right photographs that will accent the best parts of your home online. Again, that's what I will do. Mr. Max won't screen buyers, and he won't be the one answering all your questions. That's the job of the agent you hire. That's why I say, don't hire anyone because of the brokerage they work for. Hire an agent because of what they will do for you."

Being a part of the right brokerage makes a great career choice even better. Working with a strong team makes generating leads much easier while providing the training and support we all need.

But those things are not important to the seller. They want to find an agent who will maximize the exposure of their home and sell it for the most money and the best terms possible. It is up to each one of us to establish our own individual credibility to show them that we are up to that challenge.

4

MARKETING TO WIN

The *Oxford New World Dictionary* defines a salesperson as one "whose job involves selling or promoting commercial products." Notice the job description: selling *or* promoting. *Or,* like there is a choice. For those of us who sell real estate, it's not *or.* It's *and.* But in the opposite order. We promote, *then* we sell. That is why from the moment we start a listing interview, we must convince the seller that we are both the best salesperson for their home and the best marketer. The two go hand in hand.

Back when I first started in real estate, I was told that if I priced a house right, buyers would come to me. The only problem with that is there are a lot of homes out there that are priced right. Our listings will get lost in the shuffle unless we do something to make them stand out. The better we can do this and communicate to the seller why our strategy is the best, the more powerful our listing presentations will become. For us, before we can sell, we have to promote, but before we can promote, we have to win that listing. A great marketing plan is often the difference between victory and defeat.

A Different Mindset

The dictionary has several definitions for an agent. Our profession falls under the one that says, "A person or company that provides a particular service, typically one that involves organizing transactions between two other parties: a travel agent/shipping agent/*real estate agent.*" Technically, this is true. We broker the transaction of buying and selling a house. But when I look closely at what we *actually* do both as salespeople and marketers, I think our job comes a lot closer to the working definition of a completely different type of agent: a sports/entertainment agent.

A star athlete's or actor's agent does more than negotiate their client's next contract. Their agents aggressively work to find their clients the best deals on the best projects. Athletes love off-field endorsements. They want the Subway money and the Pizza Hut money and the Nike and Adidas money. Rather than wait for those companies to notice their clients, a good aggressive agent initiates endorsement deals, working the phones, making contacts, selling their client. An actor's agent doesn't wait for the studio to call with a new part in a movie. A good agent stays in constant contact with the studio decision makers through phone calls, emails, and in-person visits to land their clients the best parts with the best money and terms. After all, the agent gets paid only when the client signs a deal.

That sounds exactly like the job we do. We are agents, *real estate* agents, and our listings are our stars. Most sellers do not see our work in that light. They see us only as the ones who take a few photos of their house and put their home online and on the MLS.

We arrange to have a "for sale" sign placed in their yard, and we sit through the open house and show prospective buyers around. At the time of closing we sit down at the table with them and hand them a lot of forms to sign. Obviously, we do all of that, but I guarantee a prospective seller's understanding of who we are and what we do does a complete 180 when we use the analogy of a sports/entertainment agent. The whole idea has a very glamorous, almost mysterious, quality to it. Most of the people for whom we will work have never had an agent themselves. Having an agent means hitting the big time, and that's what we are about to deliver to them.

Great agents use a lot of different tools to maximize the exposure of their clients and increase their earning potential, and we do the same. Over the next several chapters we will explore the primary marketing tools I pitch to prospective sellers in my listing presentation. We need a lot of different tools in our marketing toolbox because we never know which will connect with a buyer. And that's what marketing is all about: connecting. The word *agent* can also be defined as a substance that brings about a chemical or physical effect. That's what we are shooting for in our marketing. We want to create an urge deep inside as many people as possible that tells them this is *the* house they have to see. The more excited we can make prospective buyers about the house before they ever see it in person, the more likely they are to make an attractive offer.

The same is true with the seller during the listing presentation when it comes to our marketing. I take the seller through several marketing approaches because one size does not fit all. I tell sellers how I have found buyers through social media and print and mailers and phone calls to other agents and cold calls to business managers and accountants. I've also found buyers using tools everyone uses. The key to the latter is to do the same old things better than your competition. The better you can explain this to a seller, with fluid speech and definitive tonality, the more confidence they will have in you that you can deliver the goods. By the time you get to the end of your listing presentation, sellers won't just want you to list their home. They will feel like they *need* you and only you if they are going to get maximum exposure and, therefore, top dollar.

Breaking the Rules

Taking this approach to marketing necessitates violating one of the basic tenets of real estate that has been drilled into our heads for decades: don't spend money. When I started out, veteran agents echoed this chorus: "Don't spend a dime promoting your listings if you can keep from it. You're just throwing your money away." Some of the seminars I attended preached the same chorus: "Don't spend money, but if you have to, spend as little as possible. There is no need to hire a professional photographer when you can shoot the pictures yourself. You don't need to take your brochures to a print shop when you can use the office copier. Good enough is good enough."

In the beginning, I followed this creed. I had no money to spend anyway, which made this advice sound that much better. But one day while sitting across the table from a seller it hit me: How can I sell myself as an expert marketer and show them these grainy brochures I printed out on the office copier right before I left to come to this appointment? "I'm going to cast a wide net," I told them, but how wide of a net could I cast with such shoddy materials? This was the moment I realized that everything I send out is a reflection of me and the quality of work that I do. Words are cheap, but a quality marketing campaign is not.

Two Goals of Investing

Today I do *not* spend money on my listings. I invest it. And I tell that to sellers in every interview. I say to them,

> "When I list your home, I will invest whatever it takes to properly expose your home to find the right buyer. Mr. Seller, notice I did not say, 'I spend money.' I never spend money. Rather I *invest* it in proven marketing channels that get results!"

This language works with sellers 100 percent of the time because it's true! I'm not just blowing smoke when I tell them this. Try it yourself. As you are about to read, my entire marketing strategy is built around investing in hiring the best photographer, as well as investing in quality, professionally printed mailings and print ads and whatever else I need to do to maximize the exposure of my listings. I invest because I am doing more than spending money to promote a single listing.

All that follows in my marketing strategy has two goals. First and foremost: sell the listing. Clients hire us to sell their homes, and that must be our top priority. That is why, in every Just Listed mailer and brochure I send out, in every print ad I buy, in every social media post, I feature photos of houses, never of me. As I tell sellers, we're the agent, the house is the star. Sellers love to hear this because it is relatable and sets us apart from any other agent they may interview. Remember, the agent always stays in the background while the star is front and center. Houses sell when buyers fall for the star. I've yet to have a buyer tell me, "Oh Jordan, I hate the house, but I love you and you have such a beautiful head of hair for a fifty-six-year-old, so I'm going to buy this house anyway."

To accomplish goal number one, not only do we need to pull out every marketing tool we have, we also need to explain to the seller the *why* behind our approach. It's important to explain to a seller that our aggressive marketing plan will reach not only those who are actively searching for homes out of necessity but also those who are not actively looking to buy or not looking for homes in the area of the potential listing. Not every serious buyer spends hours upon hours scrolling through houses on Zillow like a lonely guy swiping through Tinder. Every year I sell homes to buyers who call and say, "I wasn't really looking to make a move right now, but my wife and I have always said, if we come across the right house, we'll buy it. And then we opened up *Dream Homes Los Angeles* . . ." Many of these buyers have long had a dream neighborhood where they were just waiting for a home to come up for sale. Or they've always wanted a house that's just a little bit bigger and has that open concept they see on all the real estate shows. I also sell homes every year to those looking in a completely different part of the city who just happen to come across one of my listings through a print ad or on my Instagram account. Some of these buyers scroll through homes daily on all the real estate sites, but they never look in my listing's zip code. We must have tools to reach those buyers and explain these tools to potential clients in every listing interview.

My second goal in my marketing/investing strategy is to build my brand recognition, which will lead to more listing opportunities. Very few of us are lucky enough to star in a hit reality TV show on Bravo or Netflix. We need to build our brand through other channels, and the best way I have found is through effectively marketing our listings. The greatest compliment I ever receive during an interview is to hear a seller tell me, "Jordan, I see your name everywhere. Every time I pick up a magazine, I see a beautiful house with your name and number below it. You sure represent your listings well." A famous friend and client of mine whom I have publicly represented on many occasions once told me that I should be the mayor of Los Angeles because everywhere he goes, people tell him they're friends with me. In my eyes, that's mission accomplished, and it is even sweeter because, as I wrote before, I never put my photo in any of my print marketing unless the publication requires it. But when you expand the boundaries of your marketing strategy and stretch your net wide, people become aware of you. This not only builds your brand; it builds your career. And that's something worth investing in.

This approach to real estate is long term. Money spent marketing a listing today will not always produce a sale. But if you can deliver a sensational listing presentation with confidence and follow through by doing what you have promised, there's a 100 percent chance that in due time you will have opportunities you would not have had otherwise. Obviously, this is not something to discuss with sellers, but effective marketing with a wide net is the best way to build a brand and a career.

Reaching these two goals requires a toolbox full of tools and strategies from photographs to mailers to print ads, along with the internet and social media. When we then go into the listing interview, we bring all of these tools with us. But I have found it is not enough to run down a list of what we plan to do. Sellers' eyes light up when we explain *how* we plan to use each tool and *why* our approach will bring them the most money and the best terms. We never know which of our marketing tools will most resonate with the seller. In the following five chapters we will explore each of my favorite marketing tools beginning with one of the most basic tools in our toolbox, possibly the most obvious: epic photography. Don't laugh. There are ways to utilize great photography beyond the usual and, better yet, ways to sell your expertise on photography to the seller at the time of the interview

After photography we will explore how to leverage your social media presence in the listing interview. This chapter will not explore how to build your social media presence. We will do that later in chapter 15, where I bring in a couple of surprise guests who share their expertise.

Following social media I devote a chapter to print ads. And yes, print still works. The experts may all tell us that print is dead. Thankfully, the people who buy homes from me every year because of print have not yet received that memo.

From print we will move to Just Listed and Just Sold mailers. Mailers are one of the oldest tools available to us, but just because they are old does not mean their time has passed. In this chapter we will look at how Just Listed mailers can be elevated to reach buyers and to expand your brand.

The final chapter in the marketing section of my listing presentation will explore very effective marketing tools that do not cost us a dime, but they do call for a significant investment of time. This is the part of my presentation where I bring home the sports/entertainment agent analogy. Sellers love it.

No matter which marketing tool I am talking about in my listing presentation, I speak with confidence, conviction, and passion. I know my marketing plan works, but that's not enough to win the listing. The seller needs to catch my confidence. They need to feel my energy and excitement. Remember, excitement is contagious. Sellers need to be as sure about us as we are sure about ourselves. That is why through every step of the marketing section of our presentations, we need to convey enthusiasm as well as explain how each step works.

Now, do I always use all the marketing tools I have laid out to the seller? No, but I am always willing and plan on it if necessary.

I always hire a photographer for epic pictures of the home. And I always post my listings on my personal MLS, which is my Instagram page. I also do the prelaunch email and social media blast. Many times this is enough. A listing will sell so quickly that there is no time to do print ads or mailers for that particular listing. But I still use those tools on enough of my listings that they still work to build my brand and establish or expand my geographical farm. I am not being disingenuous with the seller when I talk about using all of these tools. I've yet to have a seller be upset that their home sold so fast for top dollar that I did not have time to put an ad for it in a real estate magazine.

I also do not always talk about every one of my marketing tools in my listing presentation. Remember, I cater my presentation to the seller. I try to get a sense from them which tool in my toolbox will resonate with them, and I go straight to it. Like money on a vacation, it's always better to have more than you need than to run out halfway through.

Nor do I believe my list of tools to be exhaustive. You may have marketing techniques and strategies that work for you that I've never thought about. If so, wonderful. I do not pretend to know everything there is about winning a listing interview. Use what works for you. The only piece of advice I offer is, when you bring that tool out of your marketing toolbox, talk about it with confidence and passion, and explain why this tool is so effective. We must never take anything for granted when it comes to selling ourselves in the listing interview. I find it is better to overexplain than to assume the seller gets it and end up losing that listing.

Before We Move On

One final note before we dive into specific marketing tools: when I was a new agent, something here might have caused me to toss this book aside without finishing it. All this talk of investing in photography and print ads and the rest would have left me discouraged because back then, I didn't have any money to invest. I couldn't afford to hire a photographer, and I didn't have the money to buy ad space. I put together Just Listed brochures, but they looked nothing like mine do today. With no money to have them professionally printed, I made copies on the office Xerox machine. Postage cost too much, so I hand delivered them to the homes in the surrounding neighborhoods and to the top buyers' agents in my area. Social media may be free today, but it didn't exist back then. I had to live by the real estate mantra of Don't Spend Money, because I had no money to spend.

Many of you reading this today may find yourselves in the same boat. Please, keep reading. Every marketing strategy that follows came out of those days when I had to find creative ways to promote my listings. I couldn't afford a photographer, so I practiced and practiced with a camera until my shots were at least as good as anyone else's out there. Thankfully, in the preinternet days, there was no way to add photos to the MLS. We needed only a shot of the front of the house for print ads or the newspaper if we chose to do so. I could not afford print ads, but I found other ways, *free* ways, to get my listings noticed. Postage cost more than I could afford back then, but going door to door with Just Listed brochures helped me build my geographic farm. And making phone calls to local buyers' agents cost then what it does now, nothing at all beyond the monthly phone bill.

My point is, if you are just starting out or if you work in a market where you have to keep costs low because your margins are so slim, what follows can still work for you, both to build your brand and to win listings! Get creative where you have to get creative, and choose wisely where to invest. But at the end of the day, these tools, when explained clearly and confidently to the seller, will help you win more listings. The ways you use them may be different than what I do, but the results can be the same. Believe me, I've been where you are. What follows over the next five chapters helped push me to where I am today.

5

USING PHOTOGRAPHY TO WIN LISTINGS

When we step inside a home for a listing interview, only one question matters: Why should this seller list with me instead of someone else? Many of us hope the answer comes down to familiarity. Since I coached the sellers' oldest daughter's soccer team last fall, surely they'll list with me. If we have nothing more to offer than what every other agent offers, perhaps coaching a team of seven-year-olds will push us over the top. But I doubt it. In my experience, I have found sellers are looking for far more than familiarity when it comes to entrusting the sale of their most valuable asset. They're looking for expertise, for professionalism, for someone whose skill set puts them above and beyond everyone else. Most sellers won't come right out and say this in so many words. They don't have to. It's understood. If we need shoulder surgery, we want the best orthopedic surgeon we can find. If our car starts making a strange noise, we take it to an expert mechanic we trust to fix it right the first time. And when it comes to selling our home, we want the best real estate agent/marketer in town who will get us top dollar and the best terms. Anyone can *say* they are the best. The question is, how can we *show* we are the best in a way that is both authentic and convincing?

So what does all of this have to do with photography? In a word, everything.

Twenty years ago real estate "photography" consisted of one or two shots of the front of a house, which may or may not be used in print ads or included in a brochure of all our listings. Today, if you post a listing with a single photograph of the front of a house, every potential buyer looks at it and immediately assumes we have to be hiding something hideous inside the home. Photographs alone will not sell a house, but you can't move listings today without them. More than 90 percent of all buyers spend their time scrolling through real estate sites. They study the photos of any home that catches their eye before they decide to go see it in person, if they even get that far. With online 3-D tours, some buyers look at us as an afterthought. With the proliferation of "for sale by owner" listings, many sellers have reached the same conclusion.

Again, what does all of this have to do with showing sellers we are expert marketers and salespeople? Once again, everything.

Epic photography doesn't just sell listings. *It sells us* to potential clients. Our chance to make a great first impression with a seller does not come when we walk through the door of their home. Instead, it comes when they google our names and click on our website, Instagram, or Facebook pages. And when they do, what do they see? The old way of thinking dictates that these pages are a place to establish our credibility with a long paragraph or two talking all about us, our experience and our successes. I recommend a different approach. Go to jordancohen.com or check out my Instagram page, @jordancohen1. You won't find personal photos or a not so brief bio of me. Instead, you will immediately see incredible photographs of several of my current listings. That's my opening statement of who I am and the quality of my work. You might think it would be difficult to take a bad photo of some of these listings given their location and the view around the home, but you would be wrong. The time of day, the angles, the use of video, the purpose behind every photo, all of it is designed to set me apart and back up my personal mantra: Serious about selling? Interview Jordan Cohen . . . you will be glad you did!

And that's why I have included a chapter about something as basic as photography in my book. This is not a tutorial on how to take better photographs for your listings. I hire a professional real estate photographer for that. Instead, this chapter is about how to use epic photography to win listing interviews. Period. The quality of the photographs is only the first part of the equation. Even more important is the explanation of why our approach makes a home stand out above the competition. To do this we need to step back and look at this section of the listing presentation through the eyes and ears of the seller. Remember, the big question we must answer is, why should they list with us rather than someone else. How we explain our approach to photography can be the difference between winning and losing this listing.

Time of Day Matters

After establishing my credibility with the seller, the marketing section of my listing presentation begins with:

"Now Mr. Seller, I'd like to get into exactly what I am going to do from A to Z, beginning to end, to maximize the exposure of your home. Fair enough?"

I then add a nod of my head. They always say yes. I then continue with:

"The first thing I will do is hire the best photographer in the business, a real estate specialist, to come and take pictures of your home. A lot of agents shoot their photos in the middle of the day, rain or shine, but I do something a little different. I have found I will get the best shots with the best lighting of your home by shooting at dusk. My photographer shoots photos of your home, both inside and out, before the sun goes down, as it is going down, and right after it sets. I've found that taking photos at dusk, with all your lights on, makes your home pop off the screen. Even the interior photos look better at dusk because there's no glare coming in from outside. Believe me, these photos will make your home stand out against other active listings, which in today's day and age of internet, social media, and print, is critical in generating interest, excitement, and that spark of momentum necessary to entice a qualified buyer to view your home in person."

Notice how I make three definitive statements above. First, I state the obvious: I'm going to photograph your home, which I will later post on the internet and social media and use in print. I don't go into all the different shots and angles I will use, because whatever I say will not be unique to me. We're all going to take inside and outside shots. We will all take different angles of the kitchen and the family room and at least some of the bedrooms. Again, this is Real Estate 101, but we have to say it to at least let the seller know photography day is coming. Before that day arrives, we will coach them to clear all the kitchen and bathroom counters and declutter (and, yes, I run into these things in multimillion-dollar listings).

If I stop with the obvious, all I have done is checked off one of the boxes of items to cover in a listing interview, but I have done nothing to stand out. That brings me to my second statement: I bring a different approach to shooting photographs. Other agents drop by to shoot photos in the middle of the day regardless of the weather. I hire a professional and we shoot the house at dusk. Hiring a professional photographer who specializes in real estate tells the seller that we are willing to invest whatever it takes to sell their home for top dollar. Shooting at dusk produces a different effect than the average real estate photo.

Sellers might find this different approach interesting, perhaps even intriguing, but so far it sounds like I am being different for the sake of being different. That brings me to the third and most important statement: I do photographs in a specific way to make them stand out from every other listing, and when it comes to selling our approach to the seller, getting noticed by buyers is all that matters. The explanation of the why behind the how demonstrates to the seller that we are experts at marketing their home. They don't have to take my word for it. When I show them the photos of my listings, they can see the difference for themselves.

It's funny, even in the luxury market that I work, I still see amateur and horrific photographs. Whenever I come across one, I call my assistant, Kristi, into my office and we both have a good laugh. But then we always end up shaking our heads in disbelief that some agents market their homes with such terrible photos. The poor sellers obviously do not realize that bad photography can cost them a fortune when the perfect buyer moves on to the next listing. In fact, one of my favorite Instagram pages is

@BadRealEstatePics. Check it out. Hopefully one of your listings never gets posted there.

Don't Take Anything for Granted

I've had listing interviews where I didn't have to say much more than this to win the listing. That's the power of epic photography in the listing presentation. But I still have more to say. I tell the seller:

> "When I return with my photographer, we are going to take a lot of pictures. After selling as many homes as I have, I understand exactly which photos will entice a buyer to come see your home as well as which photos will cause buyers to move on to the next. We will not take any pictures of a bathroom that shows the toilet. Nor will we take any pictures of an overstuffed closet. I stress that sometimes less is more."

This is exactly what I do and say, and sellers love it and appreciate it. Again, sounding professional and experienced at what works and delivering it with confidence is half the battle. I then continue:

> "I will personally choose the right angles that I know will work. You will never see a photo of one of my listings where half the photo is the street in front of the house or a side angle shot where three-quarters of the photo is the garage. I also choose the correct camera orientations for all the different media where I plan to market your home. Horizontal mode works best in the MLS and sites like Zillow and vertical for social media. There is a substantial difference in what works best, and I will be sure to get it right.

"I will be sure to choose the very best photos that I know will perform best on social media as well as those that are ideal for print and internet. As a successful real estate agent who works with various buyers and sellers, I am an expert at what is most effective in accomplishing our goals."

Everything I just told the seller may seem obvious to those of us in the business, but it could be brand new information to the seller. And that's why I go into so much detail. Doing so allows me to connect with the seller. Nearly every person who puts their house on the market has already started looking at houses online. They've scrolled through shots of kitchens with so much clutter that the countertops disappear. When we mention overstuffed closets, they relate because they have most likely taken a house off their list because the walk-in closet in the primary bedroom looks too small. I've actually seen looks of relief during this part of my presentation. Sellers want to work with an expert when it comes to the proper use of photos, and they cannot know this about us unless we explain our approach. You are the professional. Make sure sellers know this. Don't assume anything is obvious.

The Point of It All

I wrap up talking about photographing the home as I tell the seller:

"Please understand that we're going to take a lot more photos than we will use. Mr. Seller, I'm sure you've probably looked at photos of houses online. You can only scroll through so many photos until you get bored, or even worse, see a photo that is dark or cluttered that immediately makes you move on to the next house. Could you see how this could happen?"

The seller usually not only agrees but many times will say something like, "Oh yeah. I hate clicking on a home with twenty-seven angles of the same room."

"I do, too. When I launch my marketing campaign for your home, my philosophy more times than not is less is more. I am not trying to sell your home based purely on the photographs or videos. Just like a movie trailer, I want to give potential buyers just enough to get them excited to see your home in person. That's the key. I want them to see it in person so I can 'sell' it."

With this language the seller now understands the ultimate purpose behind the photographs we take and how we use them. Photographs on Zillow or Instagram or in a Just Listed mailer or wherever else we place them are the movie trailer for the home. We are not trying to sell a home through photographs alone. Instead, we want to entice buyers to come see the sellers' home in person where we can sell it. Everything in our marketing strategy comes back to this one purpose. Photographs alone will not sell a home, but when done poorly, they can make a buyer drop a house off their list without ever bothering to come to a showing. That is why it is imperative that the seller sees us as an expert who knows how to grab a buyer's attention.

The Right Shots of the Right Places

I continue my presentation with:

"That is why it is imperative for potential buyers to come tour your home personally with me or my showing agent [or assistant if you do not show homes yourself], so that I/we can point out all the great features you love so much, overcome objections, answer their questions, and most important, justify our price. I can more often than most close the sale. I'm a salesman, and to do that I need to get a buyer here, inside your home.

"I know there are exceptions to every rule, but I have never had anyone buy a home strictly because of the photographs. But the opposite can and does happen. You've probably done it yourself. You find a house that looks like it may be what you're looking for, but if the photos make one of the bedrooms look too small, you swipe left to the next house. That is why I make sure buyers only see the photographs we want them to see. Does this make sense?"

They always say it does because I have carefully explained exactly *what* I plan to do with the photographs, and *the purpose* behind my actions. This may seem like a small point, but in the eyes of the seller, explaining the purpose is the difference between an aggressive and passive marketing strategy. Sellers want someone who will aggressively try to sell their home. I know this approach works because time after time I have had sellers tell me, "All the other agents said they were going to photograph my home, but Jordan was the only one who explained how he was going to do it and why the right photographs used the right ways is so important." Taking the extra step to explain rather than assume is the difference between winning and losing a listing, and that's why we are there.

Also, keep in mind that everyone is an amateur photographer. Everyone likes to take pictures with their camera or phone. *Everyone* knows the difference between a good photograph and a bad one. Feel free to talk about photos in your listing presentation. It is relatable and familiar. You will be surprised at how this tool in your toolbox will be remembered and appreciated at the time the sellers make their final decision on which agent they will hire.

One Final Word for Brokers Only

One of the hot tools many sellers insist upon are online 3-D tours of the home. For me, spending the extra money to set up the 3-D tool does not cross the threshold into investing. I see it as wasted money. Here's why. As real estate agents, we want to invest in those things that we know will either lead to a sale or build our brand or both. In my experience, 3-D tours and posting online floor plans of homes actual deter people from coming and seeing a listing in person. Some 3-D companies actually list fewer showings as one of the advantages of giving people a virtual option. I guess that might be true if we simply let potential buyers wander through a home aimlessly and hope they happen to see all the features that make the home perfect for them without any input from us. As you will discover in a later chapter, I believe in showing my listings myself, or at the very least, having an in-depth conversation with the buyers' agent to make sure they are aware of the best features of the house. All of our marketing tools should work together with one goal in mind: bringing qualified buyers into our listings so that we can go to work selling them that home. That's where our investment should go. Rather than spending a few thousand dollars for a 3-D tour program, we would be better off investing that money in a better photographer or Just Listed mailings that will blow people away.

I realize that many times, the sellers are the ones who want to include 3-D tours and floor plans. During listing interviews, some have nearly insisted that I include one or both. Sellers have seen them while they search for their next home, and they want it for theirs. Most of the time they change their mind when I point out that the very reason why they like this online feature as a buyer is exactly why we should not use it as a seller. Buyers use them to save time by eliminating houses without actually seeing them in person. That's the last thing we want to have happen when we list a house. I explain to sellers that many buyers will dismiss that eight-by-ten secondary bedroom as too small for their two-year-old child and move on to the next listing. But if we can get them to come see the home in person, with all of its incredible features, they will love the rest of the house so much that they can find a way to make one smallish bedroom work. Again, getting a potential buyer to come see our listings in person is the ultimate goal of all our marketing strategies. I do my absolute best to avoid anything that gets in the way of this goal.

6

TAPPING INTO THE POWER OF SOCIAL MEDIA

(with Broke Agent Media's
Eric Simon and Matt Lionetti)

love Instagram as a marketing tool. Ten years ago, who would have believed a simple photo-sharing app could generate leads, build a brand, and sell houses right in the palm of the hand? I know that comes as a surprise to those of us who look at Instagram, TikTok, Facebook, and other social media platforms as nothing more than ways to share vacation videos or spout off our opinion on whatever societal ill has us worked up that day. Not me. Social media, and especially Instagram, has become my favorite marketing tool, not only for my listings but for my brand. Posting daily on

Insta reaches more people on a personal level than all the potato chip bag clips I could pass out or all the signs along the outfield fence of the local high school baseball field I could buy.

The personal touch is what sets social media apart. Of all the marketing tools we can use, this is the most relatable. Those we are trying to reach consume this content on their phones multiple times a day. When they like what they see and share it with their friends, it's like they become part of our marketing team for free! Like any other tool, your listings won't immediately sell the moment you post them on your Instagram or Facebook page. Social media doesn't work like that. Instead, we need to think of it as part of a long-term strategy to build our brand while promoting our listings. Unlike other tools we might use, social media never sleeps, and it stretches beyond oceans while also reaching across town. It is not an overstatement to say that social media is the future of our business. Ignore it and odds are pretty good that we'll end up going the way of the dinosaurs.

Social media is more than a big picture marketing strategy. I find it is a very effective tool to bring out during my listing presentation. But do not expect a seller to be dazzled when we tell them we plan to put their home on all our social media accounts. The key is to tell them why we plan to market their home through social media and how this will help find a buyer. You may have thousands of Instagram followers, but if all we do is tell the seller how many followers we have, it won't take them long to figure out that our thousands of followers do not automatically mean thousands of potential buyers for *their* home. We have to explain how this tool will benefit them.

Separating Ourselves from the Pack

Immediately after presenting my approach to photography, I say,

"Mr. Seller, as I told you, I want to explain to you from A to Z how I plan to market your home. Getting the right photographs is crucial, and so is using them in an effective way. Now, obviously, your home will appear with my name attached on the internet real estate sites including Zillow, Realtor.com, and all the rest. I plan to feature the best photos I have personally selected that accentuate the best features of your home, as well as an incredible description of your home I will write myself. Every other agent you interview may not go the extra mile like me to make your home stand out on these sites, but believe me, every agent will have your home on Zillow and the rest. It doesn't take any extra effort to put your home on those sites because the moment I upload your home onto the Multiple Listing Service, every real estate site automatically uploads it.

"That is why I am not going to waste thirty or forty-five minutes of your time selling you on Zillow and Realtor.com. Of course, these sites are extremely effective tools for marketing a home, but what I want to do in the brief time we have is show you everything I do *above and beyond* the real estate sites."

Every agent we go up against will talk about the popular real estate sites, which is why I go ahead and address the elephant in the room. But I do it in a way that shoots down the idea that it takes some sort of marketing genius to land a listing on them. My strategy in the interview is always to try to set myself apart from the pack while also doing the same things everyone else does—but better. That's why I do not waste the little time I have in the listing interview by going into great detail about a tool that even "For Sale by Owner" listings land on. Instead, I move quickly to the tool I have found to be especially effective. I tell the seller,

"Mr. Seller, I am a big believer in social media marketing, especially Instagram. Are you on Instagram yourself?"

Most people will say yes. From time to time, however, someone says no. For them, I will briefly stop and explain what Instagram is and how it works before continuing:

"Fantastic. Then you know how Instagram is a very visual platform, which is why I will select very specific photos and create epic videos of your home that will look best on this medium. I find Instagram to be such a great tool not just because it shows your home in the best possible way but also because of its reach. Real estate sites like Zillow and Realtor.com work great for potential buyers who are looking for a home in your specific neighborhood. But what about those who are not? I have had great success with Instagram in exposing my properties to people who may not be looking for a home in your exact area but close, or maybe not even be actively shopping for a home at all but would be if they became aware of your home somehow. The latter are those who always say that if they ever came across the right home, they'd buy it. Instagram delivers that home, your home, right to them on their phone or tablet.

"Through strategic hashtags and reels, I also use Instagram to reach buyers who may be unaware of your neighborhood. Many of these are buyers relocating from other parts of the country and even from overseas. They are not familiar with the great neighborhood in which you live, which is why they will never stumble across your home while scrolling through pages of houses on real estate sites. But many will find it on my Instagram page. I know this works because I sell homes every year this way."

When I start talking about Instagram, the sellers can hear the enthusiasm in my voice because I truly believe in it. Some of my best clients who have become close friends found me through it, including WWE superstar the Miz and his wife, Maryse. The two of them had relocated from Texas to Southern California. They rented a home in Calabasas for a year. When they decided to make the move permanent and buy a home, they looked there because they loved Calabasas. That changed when the Miz came across my Instagram account where he saw one of my listings, a beautiful home in Westlake Village. Even though it was only ten minutes from Calabasas, they had never considered it before. The Miz sent me a direct message asking about the home. I called him, got him and his wife excited over the phone, and scheduled a time for them to see it. They didn't love that house, but they loved the area. Eventually I found them exactly what they were looking for in Westlake Village. Like I said, this happens for me several times every year.

This story, in particular, gets better still. The home I sold the Miz and Maryse is now famous. It appears in almost every episode of the hit show *Miz and Mrs* on the USA Network. If not for Instagram, I might never have sold them their mega estate. More than that, I would not have met such *awesome* friends.

I continue on with my presentation by saying,

"Back when I first started selling real estate, the only way for us to find other agents' listings came through the Multiple

Listing Service or MLS. Even then, the only people who could see it were other real estate agents. Today, my Instagram page is like my own personal MLS. Other agents see it, but so do hundreds of thousands or even millions of others. I've sold homes to buyers who had never even heard of Instagram, much less used it. I remember one client in particular whose daughter's friend happened to come across one of my listings on my Instagram page. She told her friend's parents, 'Mr. and Mrs. Jones, I know you are not really looking at houses in North Ranch, but isn't this a great looking home?' They agreed, called me, and I sold the house to them. That's the power of social media that I plan to put to work for you."

Every listing interview is different because sellers are all different. You never know which tool in the toolbox is going to move the seller from thinking about listing with you to being convinced they *must* list with you. More and more I find that explaining how and why I plan to use the power of social media to sell a home is that tool. Perhaps it is the most relatable. Remember, before we arrive at the listing interview, the seller has already googled us. If we have Instagram, they've already found our pages. They've also looked through other real estate sites and scrolled through dozens and dozens of photographs. When they compare what they see on the typical real estate site to our Instagram pages, they should see a huge difference.

Remember, no one is going to buy a home simply because they saw it on Instagram. The goal is to pique potential buyers' interest just enough to have them come see the property in person. Walking into an interview where the seller has already experienced this on my page themselves makes convincing them to list with me that much easier, especially after I explain why I do what I do and how I can use this to market their home. Like every other aspect of this part of my listing presentation, telling a seller what you are going to do is not enough. We must explain how this approach will help find that buyer who is willing to pay their price or more.

How Can I Build a Social Media Presence That Will Win Listings?

I realize that everything you just read may overwhelm some readers because not everyone reading this book is up to date on the most effective ways to use social media as a marketing tool. I would guess nearly all of us already have some sort of social media presence. Since I know of ninety-year-old great-grandmothers who have Facebook pages, the odds are pretty good the average real estate agent does, too. You don't exactly need a computer science degree from MIT to use something like Instagram. I am the least tech-savvy dinosaur you will find, and I use social media every day. But simply having an Instagram or Facebook page is worlds away from utilizing its full power to build your brand and leveraging it as a tool that helps win listings.

Effectively tapping into the power of social media demands we do more than throw in the occasional post about a new listing. So where do we start to turn an app we normally use to share photos of our dog into an effective marketing tool? I'm not the guy to ask . . . but I know who is.

Eric Simon, founder of Broke Agent Media, and real estate agent, comedian, and social media maven Matt Lionetti are the best I know when it comes to explaining how to establish a social media presence that will build your business. If you don't already follow them on Instagram, you need to go to @thebrokeagent and @matt.lionetti right now and click the follow button. These two guys are hilarious, but they are also geniuses when it comes to how to stay on the leading edge of the ever-evolving world of social media. Their website, www.brokeagentmedia.com, is filled with podcasts, interviews, training courses, and even free ebooks on how to use social media in real estate. Social media is always evolving and changing, sometimes from week to week. I highly recommend the Broke Agent site and their resources as a way to keep up. I am grateful they have graciously agreed to share a few of their insights in the second half of the chapter. We only scratch the surface here. For more, check out their books and resources. You'll be glad you did.

So my first question for Eric and Matt is simply, where do you start? How can the average agent go from posting vacation photos for friends on Instagram to establishing an online presence that effectively promotes both their listings and themselves?

Eric: You start by warping your thought process around the idea that posting to social is not a hobby. It is not a waste of time. When done right, posting on social media is synonymous with door knocking and cold-calling, except you reach a more massive audience.

Matt: Eric is right. Every social post is like setting up little digital real estate signs on people's phones and in their heads. Even the stories in your feed not directly related to real estate create familiarity with you as a real estate agent in the minds of your followers. There's a famous quote out there that says a post that gets a hundred thousand views is like knocking on ten thousand doors a day. That's the power of social media right there.

Eric: And it doesn't stop working when the day ends. When I'm cold-calling, the moment I hang up the phone, I'm done. But when I post a reel or a video, it stays out there 24/7. I've even had people reach out to me from a video that I posted five months earlier.

That's what I love about social. It's a way to have content constantly working for you 24/7/365. And the content doesn't just reach out to potential clients. Matt gets a lot of referrals from other agents through his Instagram account. This simply means that the more informative you are, the more you build your brand and your reputation, the more others in the industry will follow you, which helps your business.

Jordan: I learned this by trial and error. I used to post lots of photos of me and my wife and kids. No one cared. I had no audience engagement. But when I started focusing on posting epic photos and videos of the luxury homes I list, along with strategic hashtags, not only did my number of followers jump, people shared my posts and replied both to the post and with direct messages. It didn't take long for me to figure out that I had tapped into an audience that loves seeing beautiful homes in amazing settings. Now the vast majority of my posts feeds that audience. Occasionally I'll post something personal just to humanize my page, something like a photo of my family and me at a Rams game or my dog on the beach, but mainly I give my audience what they come to my page to see.

Matt: I 100 percent agree with you. You need to know who your audience is, and you won't until you make some mistakes. It's all trial and error. When I first started posting, one week I'd post a video and it would do great. Lots of comments. Lots of shares. The next week I'd post another video and it didn't get any love. Instead of quitting, I stopped and asked why one did so well and the other didn't. The more this happened, the more I learned how to tailor my content to my audience, which is also key to growing an audience. Eric and I, we focus on humor related to real estate. Over time we've learned what people want to see. Those early videos that didn't do so well were actually the best thing that could have happened.

Eric: We had a guest on our podcast a while back who said the two most important ways for real estate agents to create content and provide value that keeps an audience coming back is to either entertain or educate. I think we are in a unique space in real estate to provide both. Matt and I entertain with humor. Jordan does it with the visuals he provides of dream properties. If you aren't funny, and most real estate agents aren't, and if you don't work in a luxury market with homes overlooking the Pacific Ocean, and most of us don't, you can still provide value. People want to be educated about real estate. They want to know more about the inspection process. They want to know which sales tactics work and which do not. They want to learn how to get their first invest-ment property. All of this gives us an opportunity to provide con-tent that connects with an audience.

Matt: You also have to keep your eye on the big picture. I think most agents are too worried about selling on Instagram. That's not how social media works. Every time I post I am trying to start conversations, which is why you have to be authentic. Very rarely will I post something and someone messages me and says, "Hey Matt. We want you to list our house." But they do message me and start conversations. And those conversations are now leads, and like any lead, we have to nurture them over months and months. We've all heard it a thousand times that real estate is a long-term game. Social is no different. You will not get fifty sales the day after you post a viral video. But as conversations start, I learn more about my leads. After seeing me wear a Ramones T-shirt in a video, I may get a comment that says, "Oh man. I love the Ramones." I make a note of that. A couple weeks later when I see another post about the Ramones, I send it to them to keep the conversation going. Time and time again, the conversation eventually turns when they say, "By the way, Matt, we're looking to sell our house in the next two months. Can we talk to you about listing it?"

Jordan: I get listing interviews and sales the same way.

Eric: Your social media presence is your digital business card. When you look up someone online, the first thing that pops up is their social media. When they see some of your personal touches, people relate to that, and it gives you a slight advantage. I think of social media as a way of building relationships with people. The more they get to know you, the more they come to trust you and relate to you. When you post videos, you start popping into people's heads. Like I said before, it's like setting up little digital real estate signs on people's phones and in their heads.

Matt: Social humanizes everything for me. When I post a video, a lot of the response I get is, "Matt, we feel like we know you." That's why I use video. I think it's a great tool for agents, especially newer agents who don't have a large pool from which to draw referrals. Social is a great way for people to feel like they know you, and it is way easier to call someone you know than a stranger. That's how I get listing appointments. It is much easier and effective than cold-calling and door knocking.

Jordan: This brings me to a question I get nearly every day through Instagram from other agents. They all ask, "I don't understand why I don't have more followers. What do I have to do to get more?" A lot of times I go to their pages, and part of the answer is staring right back at me. I see bad photos of ugly houses. Or I see poorly lit photos of things that don't matter to buyers, like a tree out in the yard. The other thing I see is a page that's nothing but vacation photos with a bio that has a long list of the person's loves and interests before tacking on the words *part-time real estate agent* at the end. Even worse is when I find all their political views on their page. I don't mean to be cruel, but when I see this, I want to ask, "Why should more people follow you? What do you offer that will make somebody want to invest their time on your page? And what on this page tells potential buyers and sellers that you are the one they need to call when it comes to buy or sell their home?"

Eric: Your profile is the first mechanism that captures a lead. When I go to Matt's page, I find great posts, a lot of really funny stuff connected to the work we do in real estate that makes me want to follow him. I also find front and center that he's a real estate agent, where he works, and a profile photo. That's what we have to do. Our social media profile has to be optimized to capture leads.

Jordan: But what about increasing your number of followers?

Matt: The biggest trap people fall into is trying to be everything to everybody. I did that early on when I had some videos that worked and some that didn't. Here's what I found: once I niched down the content I was creating, my audience got broader, my business got broader, everything expanded. When you tailor content to a specific audience, people know what they will find when they come to your page. If you try to be everything to everybody, you get lost in the mix. But when you create specific, consistent content, pages take off. That's what I see on Jordan's Instagram page. I understand why you have so many followers because the photography and the reels you post are the best I've seen. The captions are also great. They tell us a little story, not only about the listing but also how grateful you are for your listings and your sales. It's captivating and its genuine and it attracts people to your page. I find a lot of people are scared to be themselves on social. That's weird.

Eric: And Instagram is the best place to do this and the best place to grow an audience that will build your business. Twitter is all about the 280 characters, and most people use it to air out their grievances. Facebook is still important simply because so many people are on it, but for the most part it has become more and more a place to go and argue, especially over politics. Instagram, and to a lesser degree TikTok, are the best places to host and grow an audience right now. You can do so much on Instagram that connects with people. You can do images, highlights, stories, messaging featuring links, slideshows, carousel posts, and reels, which are short-form video. You can also do long-form video, fifteen-minute podcasts, as well as massive captions that are basically blog posts. Because both Instagram and TikTok are overwhelmingly visual, they are great places to showcase real estate content. You can also tag people, which can reach those who do not follow you. TikTok has a very potent algorithm with which you can have zero followers and still post a video that gets a million views. You also want to have a uniform handle across all social media platforms so that when people search for you, they will find it all.

Jordan: You mention algorithms. How do they work in increasing your followers? A couple of years ago, I used hashtags to increase the reach of my posts. Today that doesn't work as well. Now I use a lot of reels on Instagram, which seem to be the way now to register on the algorithm, but I don't really understand how it all works. I remember when our office got its first fax machine. I was blown away. I remember asking someone, "You mean I don't have to hand deliver documents anymore? I can just put them in a machine?" Then came email, and I had no idea how that worked. Now, with social media, we're talking about algorithms and going viral and all that. How can the average agent not only make sense of it all but tap into it to build their followers?

Matt: You have to remember that it is always evolving. Jordan talked about going from hand delivering documents to fax machines to email, and now we have DocuSign. The same is true of music. Mötley Crüe released their stuff on cassette tapes, and then came CDs, and now it's all on digital download. Everything keeps evolving. And if you don't evolve, you die. So that's the first thing to keep in mind. We could put all the latest information on social media algorithms in this book, but by the time it comes out it will all be out of date.

Eric: Not to promote our own stuff, but you can take the courses at brokeagentmedia.com.

Jordan: Promote it!

Eric: We try to stay on top of all the changes. You can also hire a social media manager who can keep up on everything for you, but it is hard for someone else to capture your exact voice.

Jordan: I have toyed with the idea of hiring a social media manager but have decided to do it all myself because I believe people will notice the difference. I would never want to deceive my Instagram friends and followers. Do you agree?

Eric: Posting content yourself is the best way. You can tell from a person's feed if someone is just pumping out generic content. You need to understand that building your digital real estate brand is just as important, if not more important, than your signs and even the actual brick and mortar brokerage. Everyone's attention is on their phones. If we want to capture it, that's where we have to go. If people are looking down at their phones, why would I put an ad on a park bench or a huge billboard? How to get noticed is always changing, which means we have to always work to keep in step with it.

Matt: And stay away from divisive topics like politics and religion. People have strong opinions about those things, but I see social media as a place to have some fun.

Eric: Posting polarizing content might get you great engagement, but it is also a great way to alienate half of the population. Remember, tapping into the power of social media means trying to reach the largest number of people. You want to educate. You want to entertain. And you want people to enjoy logging on to your page.

Jordan: And when they do, they'll not only keep coming back; they'll repost your stuff and you'll reach more people, which will continually increase your reach. That's what we want to do as we promote our listings: build our brand and have a blast doing it!

7

WINNING LISTINGS WITH PRINT ADS. YES, PRINT!

M y phone rang one Sunday morning. "I'm calling about an ad you ran for a house in Calabasas," the caller said. "I'd love to see it if it is still available."

This wasn't just any of my listings. It belonged to NBA player Chris Mills, one of my first professional athlete clients. "It is and it's a great house," I said, "but if you don't mind, the seller requires that I ask a couple of qualifying questions before I can schedule a showing."

"Absolutely. No problem," the caller said.

"First off, may I please have your full name and what you do for a living?"

"Of course. My name is Gabe Kapler, and I am a professional baseball player."

That was all I needed to hear. Kapler wasn't just any baseball player, not to a guy like me who grew up in the San Fernando Valley. He was a local legend. He wasn't drafted by a major league team until the fifty-seventh round, but through hard work and determination he made it to the majors with the Tigers only three years later. He called me shortly after joining the Boston Red Sox. Now he was looking for a house in Southern California, which he called home during the off-season.

"I've got to tell you that it is a pleasure to speak with you," I said. "I grew up in the Valley, and I've been a fan of yours for a long time. When would you like to see the house?"

"I'm in town now, so as soon as you can," Gabe said.

I showed him the property the next day. Unfortunately it was not a fit for him. When he decided to pass, I followed up with, "I have other homes that I can show you." He told me he'd like that, so we spent time together looking at homes. As we did, the two of us just clicked and a friendship was born. Eventually, I found him a home in the south San Fernando Valley, but the story doesn't end there.

I have represented many famous people over the years, and I do my best to avoid asking for favors. But one day I found myself up against a huge challenge and didn't know where else to turn. I had volunteered to coach my ten-year-old son's baseball team. I figured that since I had been a pretty good player back in the day, this would be a piece of cake. But the closer we got to the first practice, the more I realized I didn't want to be another "dad" coach. I wanted to knock this out of the park for my son and his friends. I called Gabe and explained the situation. "Kap, I just volunteered to coach my son's Little League baseball team," I said, "and I haven't played baseball in twenty years. Can you give me any quick tips on how to coach these guys?"

"I'll do you one better," Gabe said. "I'm in town. Why don't you grab your mitt and your bat and ball and meet me over at Krebs Park and I'll show you?"

I was floored. The two of us spent three hours together. He showed me how to hold the bat correctly and the proper way to field a ground ball. I thought I already knew how to do these things, after all I was a Little League all-star, but as it turned out, I had it all wrong. I learned more in those three hours than I learned in twelve years of playing ball as a kid. The whole time, Gabe kept telling me, "The most important thing is for these kids to have fun, and you, too. Teach them the right techniques, but have fun with it." I took it all to heart and passed as much as I could to the boys. Our team didn't win the championship that year. We ended up finishing second; but man, the team and I sure had a blast.

Several years ago Gabe was named the manager of the Philadelphia Phillies. I was so excited for my friend. I sent him a text that said, "I'm as happy as Robert De Niro in *Goodfellas* when he found out Joe Pesci was going to get made. My friend just became a major league manager. So happy for you, man." (If you don't get the reference, you have to watch the movie. It's one of my favorites.) Gabe texted me back and said this was one of the best congratulatory messages he received.

After two years in Philly, Gabe became manager of the San Francisco Giants. As someone born and raised in LA, I've been a diehard Dodgers fan my entire life. But the minute the Giants named Gabe Kapler manager, I switched allegiances. If you know anything about sports, you understand that no real Dodgers fan will ever, ever, under any circumstances switch to being a Giants fan. But I did for one simple reason: friends always come before teams, even a team I've cheered on my entire life! To think all of this was because of an ad I ran in the paper for one of my listings in the community of Calabasas. Running print ads is like placing a bet in Vegas, and that day I hit the jackpot.

Yeah, But I Don't Gamble

Some of you after reading the previous story may be thinking, *That's great for you, Jordan, but one story doesn't change the fact that print ads are dead, and you must be a dinosaur for using them.* Let me assure you that I do not waste money on any marketing tool that doesn't produce results. I never spend money just to spend. I always invest it, and I want to invest where it is going to pay off. And print pays off. Every year I land enough sales through print ads to more than justify the relatively low cost of using this platform.

I am not going to lie to you and tell you that every ad automatically produces a sale. My phone doesn't blow up the moment a new issue of *Homes & Land* hits the street. Print is a little like buying a lottery ticket or walking into a casino. Sometimes you run the ad and nothing happens, at least nothing that you can immediately measure. That doesn't mean the ad didn't work. Remember the two purposes behind every marketing strategy I outlined in chapter 4: sell the listing by reaching as many people as possible and build your brand. Even ads that appear to bomb help check the second box, which results in future sales and listings. Other times you run an ad and you get a small payoff. Someone sees the ad, calls, but for whatever reason they do not buy the home you've listed. A month, a year, maybe even longer down the road, however, this same person calls and you end up doing a deal. I've had people call and say, "Jordan, you may not remember me, but I called you last year regarding one of your listings that I saw in *Westlake Malibu Lifestyle* magazine. That house did not work for us, but you were extremely helpful and we appreciated that. We'd like to work with you now." That's hitting the jackpot to me.

There's a bigger reason why print remains one of the tools in my marketing toolbox. Sellers who interview me have a very different view of print than most real estate trainers. When I bring out samples of my full-page, full-color magazine ads that feature photos of houses and never of me, sellers' eyes light up. It gives them something tactile they can see with their eyes and hold in their hands. I've also found that sellers like to see their own homes in ads, especially when the photograph pops off the page with just the right light and camera angle. This gives me a decided edge over any other real estate agent they may interview who either dismisses print as irrelevant or runs it down as a marketing tool whose time has passed. And isn't that the point? Print ads help me win listings. They help build my brand. And they sell houses. What more could you ask for in a marketing tool?

How to Present Print as a Marketing Tool

When I start the print section of my presentation, I begin with:

"As I told you, Ms. Seller, I'm going to do anything and everything I can to give your home maximum exposure to as many potential buyers as possible. The more people who see your home across different media, the better the odds that we will find that *one* buyer who will pay your price or more. And remember, it only takes one. I often find that one with a tool other agents may tell you is a waste of money, and that's print ads. Every year I sell homes as a direct result of print market-ing. And I can give you many examples.

"The way I utilize print works a lot like social media. I do more than advertise locally. I expand my reach to other areas throughout Southern California and beyond, especially in those areas where I know people are looking to move to a neighborhood like yours that has better schools, better ame-nities, and a better quality of life.

"Now you might ask, won't these people search this area on one of the real estate sites? Not necessarily. As with social media and Instagram, print is a great way to reach buyers who will never type your zip code into an internet search. Print also reaches the millions of people who love to pick up a pub-lication and look through it, whether while sitting at a deli or waiting for their car to be serviced, or in their home with a publication mailed directly to them. They may not even be looking for a house themselves, but they have a friend or coworker who is. Mr. Seller, don't you think there might be a 1 percent chance that one of these people will be interested in your home? I do. And that's why I will invest in print adver-tising to bring your home to them."

With this language, I have set myself apart from every agent the seller may interview who either does not mention print or who dismisses it as a waste of money. I've also explained how print has worked for me in the past and how I plan to use it for them. If I stopped here, this portion of my presentation may or may not con-vince the seller to list with me. I think most potential clients might not even hear me because what I am saying is so similar to my explanation of how I plan to use social media. That is why I go one step further. In my toolbox of marketing tools, this next step is the hammer. I continue:

"Mr. Seller, through the course of all my years selling real estate, I have narrowed down which publications work and which do not. So I have chosen and selected the following publications that I know work for me time and time again."

I then go through each publication by name. As I do, I hand a copy of each to the sellers and open to my ad. When the sellers hold the magazine in their hand and see the quality of the photography, we connect. I then explain what sets my ads apart from my competitors, other than that I always do full-page ads. If you cannot afford to do a full page, you can still use much of my wording below to make your ads stand out:

"The first thing I'd like you to notice is this is an ad for my listing, not for me. You are not hiring me to sell myself. You hire me to sell your home, which is why my photograph never appears in any of my advertisements. You will notice down at the bottom of the page I have my name, contact information, and website. Ideally, anyone interested in your home will call me or go to my website where they can see a full spread of amazing photographs of your home."

This goes against another tenet we hear in training seminars. The old way of thinking tells us to place our photograph in a prominent place in everything we do as a way of building our brand. Then people will recognize us when we go to the grocery store or take our kids to the park to play. And if they recognize us, they may strike up a conversation about real estate, and just like that, we will land either a buyer looking for a home or a potential listing.

I get it. That can work. But for me, I stopped placing my photograph in all my marketing for one very simple reason: when I am off work, I prefer to be off work. But I soon found an added benefit.

By not featuring my photo in any of my ads, I make it clear to sellers that I am trying to sell their home, not myself. That matters to people a lot more than one might think. Ads still build my brand, but rather than associating my face with my work, people associate beautiful homes. Isn't that the way it should be?

I continue showcasing the magazine ads by saying:

"I want you to also notice that I do not have the usual, corny description of the house filled with words like *spacious kitchen* and all that sort of language I know you've probably seen a thousand times. Instead I give bullet points of your home's key features. Remember, we are not going to receive an offer on your home based on this ad alone. We want to grab their attention and have them come see it in person. That is why I use bullet points. I give them the essentials quickly and efficiently but always just enough to lure them to make that call and see your house. And that's my goal with every marketing tool I share with you. I only get paid when I sell your home, not when I list it. That is why I am going to pull out every tool I have to go aggressively after that buyer who is out there that's just waiting to find a home like yours."

Believe me, it works. If I shared every story of sales made through print, this book would end up as thick as *War and Peace*. And no, I've never read *War and Peace*, but I've heard it is really long. My point is, print works. It sells listings. It lands buyers who would never otherwise come across your listing. On top of it all, it builds your brand. I believe in it, but you have to make up your own mind about it. Just because some trainers who have never actually worked as real estate agents say print is dead doesn't make it dead. I've never been a trainer. I'm just a real estate agent who works alone with my two assistants, and print has helped build my business to where it is today. Whether you use it or not is up to you. As for me, the next time you are in the Los Angeles area, pick up a copy of *Homes & Land*. You'll most likely see a Jordan Cohen listing prominently displayed.

8

A TIME-TESTED TOOL SELLERS LOVE

Social media as a marketing tool casts a net that can literally wrap around town and around the world. Print ads bring our nets closer to home, but they still have the potential to reach every corner of our cities, sometimes our entire state and beyond. That's exactly what we want to do as real estate agents. When it comes to promoting our listings, we want to cast as wide a net as possible to reach as many potential buyers as possible. But sometimes that one buyer who will come in with the best offer and the best terms lives just around the corner from our listing. Or a homeowner in the neighborhood has a friend or relative who has been waiting for a house in your listing's neighborhood to come up for sale. Our wide nets may skip right over these potential buyers. To reach them we need a narrower focus, which brings me to the next tool in my marketing toolbox: the Just Listed brochure.

I can already hear the groans from many of you. You came to this chapter looking for a time-tested tool that will land listings, and I pull out the tired old retread from Real Estate 101 that had to be on its way out when I first started selling houses in 1990. Just Listed mailers? How about using smoke signals or Morse code to promote listings? Those seem just as timely. How can something so old and so low-tech and, frankly, so boring help me convince a seller to list with me? On top of that, aren't Just Listed postcards all about building a geographic farm? That's not exactly the sort of thing we should mention in an interview. After all, sellers want us to market their homes, not our brands. It seems like pulling out a handful of Just Listed postcards would lose listings, not win them.

All of the above is completely true . . . if you do Just Listed mailers exactly like everyone else, and why would any successful agent do that?

Just Listed postcards are probably one of the oldest tools in our toolboxes, but that doesn't mean they don't still work today. Listing interviews are won by doing the same old things *better* than your competition *and* by explaining to the seller why this ancient tool will help sell their home. Yes, Just Listed brochures build your farm. That's a great side benefit. I've received many invitations to come do a listing interview as a direct result of someone receiving one of my Just Listed brochures. After all, timing is everything. Keep in mind, when my listing interview takes place within my farm, the seller will likely already be well acquainted with my brochures. If they have seen my brochures, they already know I market homes, not myself. That may be why they contacted me about listing their home in the first place.

An Attention Grabber

My approach to Just Listed mailers is very different from the average agent's, and I point this out to the seller right from the start. I tell them:

"I'm sure you've probably received postcards from some of the local real estate agents that say "Just Listed" across the front with a photo of a house on one side and a photo of the agent on the other. You may not have noticed both photos because you probably throw them away as fast as you pull them out of your mailbox. [Insert fake laugh here.] In the business we call those Just Listed mailers. You are probably wondering how effective a tool these postcards could possibly be if they end up in the trash unread? Right?"

I nod my head.

"Believe it or not, I'm going to send out a Just Listed mailer for your home, but it is not going to end up in the trash because I don't send out postcards. Instead, I will send out an epic brochure"—I then hand them a sample mailer—"that will go to every home in your neighborhood as well as other neighborhoods that I know have a large number of people looking to move into your area. Please notice how I've strategically chosen the best photos for this format and how I highlight some of the home's best features. My goal in putting this brochure together was to send out something that's just too nice to toss without first looking through it."

Early on when I first started going up against other agents for listings, I started collecting the Just Listed mailers all the other agents and brokers sent out as a way of learning everything I could about my competition. I was looking for an edge, and it didn't take me long to find it. The typical Just Listed mailer consisted of a standard postcard with a small photo of the home on one side and an awkward photo of the agent holding a dog or pretending to be on the phone on the other. By the way, I never got this whole "on the phone" thing. Do they really believe sellers will fall for that and think to themselves, *Wow. This guy's so busy he didn't even have time to hang up the phone to get his picture taken?* I think most people's BS meter will see right through that. I also don't understand throwing the dog into the picture. Is that supposed to make them more relatable and therefore more likely to get listings? For me, the day I see an ad for a doctor or a lawyer that features them holding a dog or pretending to be on the phone, that's when I will do the same.

I also took brochures that other agents left at their listings. Most were single page, Xeroxed copies with the same photo of the house from the postcard on top. Below the photo was the price along with a bright and cheerful description of the home filled with words like *lovely* and *spacious* and *won't last long*. I then asked myself, how can I do these not just better but much better? I upped the game with a full-color, full-sized, uniquely shaped, printed brochure with multiple photos of the home. Instead of a description, I listed bullet points of the key features that I knew buyers wanted to see. I then took my ideas to my printer along with my competitors' postcards and asked him to put together something that blew the others out of the water. As I tell sellers in my listing presentation, my goal is to send out a mailer that recipients will actually look at and show their spouse rather than immediately drop in the trash as just one more piece of junk mail.

Elevating Just Listed brochures costs more than the typical Just Listed postcards, but for me, the difference is worth it. Again, these mailers are not an expense but a threefold investment. First, elevated Just Listed brochures immediately set us apart from other agents the seller may interview. Second, a mailer that looks too good to throw away with hardly a glance when it shows up in people's mailboxes can translate into buyers. The goal is to get neighbors to connect our listing to a friend or family member who might love a house like this. Finally, a high-quality Just Listed brochure will establish our names and reputation in a specific area as an agent who does things right, which then builds our geographic farms and, most likely, generates more listing interviews. Obviously, this is a place where each of us has to make a financial decision. If you sell starter homes, it doesn't make much sense to spend thousands on an elaborate mailer. But we all have to ask ourselves, *How much are we willing to invest to make ourselves a household name in a defined geographic area?*

"Why" Is More Important Than "What"

I continue my presentation:

"Let me explain the benefits of sending out these brochures to your neighborhood. First, the odds are great we will find someone in your area who is looking for a home like yours, one better than their current home. Everywhere I go, there are people who have their eye out for a specific type of house in their neighborhood. They are not actively searching Zillow or the other real estate sites, but they've told themselves that if the right house came up for sale around here, where their kids could stay in the same schools, they'd buy it. Don't you think there's a good chance that there is someone who loves living in your neighborhood but would rather live in your house? That's why I will mail everyone a Just Listed brochure, to let them know that their wait is up.

"My second reason for mailing these brochures to your surrounding area is because your neighbors who love this area probably know someone they'd like to see move here. Maybe it's grandparents who want their family closer, or maybe it's a family who wants to have their parents move nearby. Again, these people do not spend their time looking at homes online, but when they receive this mailer and see your home is available, they're going to let their friends or family know. I don't believe in waiting for someone to happen to come across your home. I want to take your home to them. And when they see the photos and they read all the features your home has to offer, they will see that this house is just what their friends or family members have been waiting for. I know these methods work. I've sold many homes simply because I introduce listings to people that never would have found them otherwise."

Remember, you should always justify what you do, and tell sellers it works. I cannot stress enough the importance of taking the extra moment to explain the purpose behind everything you do. Never take it for granted that the seller already knows why you plan to send out mailers to three to five hundred homes around them. This is about more than making sure the seller understands your actions. Explaining the reasons behind what you do also shows them that you will take a very aggressive approach to selling their home. I have found sellers prefer an aggressive agent who is going to get out there and work to sell their home over an agent who collects listings and waits for buyers to come find them. Another tagline I use often, and have been using for the past thirty years is, "Aggressive marketing . . . it works!" Feel free to try it (unless you work in my neighborhoods, ha ha). Hopefully it works for you, too.

Casting Wider

Just Listed mailers are more than a tool that works within a five-mile radius of your listing. I use them as part of the wider net I cast out. That is why I tell sellers:

"I plan to mail the Just Listed brochures to more than your neighbors. I will also mail them to my sphere of influence, including my former clients along with business managers and accountants I know who work with a wide variety of people. The odds are high that at least one of them know someone looking for a house like yours. I also send the Just Listed brochures to the relocation officers of the large employers and businesses like [insert the large companies in your area]. These companies often hire or transfer people from other states, even other countries, to our area. Obviously, their employees moving here need to find a home quickly. Mailing the Just Listed brochure on your home gives them a very attractive option.

"Finally, I will send the brochures to top agents all over the country who are well known for referring buyers to our city, agents who specialize in relocation. I have a proven database of these agents I've collected over the years. I've worked with many of them throughout my career. My job as a real estate agent is to market your home not only to the general public but also to the real estate community. Let's be honest. Busy agents, like myself, don't have time to sit on the computer all day looking for new listings. We're out there showing properties. That's why I will take your home directly to them."

Just Sold Mailers

Throughout this part of the marketing presentation, I make it clear that I am not trying to sell myself on the Just Listed brochures. The mailer is all about their home. But I also have an honest conversation with the seller in which I tell them:

> "Once I sell your home, I am going to tell the world about it because I'm always proud when a home sells. Hopefully, at the end of this process, your experience with me will exceed your expectations. If it does, I would be honored if you might give me a short testimonial about your experience that I can use. You might think of this like a review on Amazon, but I've been doing this since long before Jeff Bezos ever sold his first book online. For me, sending out these Just Sold mailers is a lot of fun. It's a way for all of us to celebrate the exciting news that your home sold for a great price."

Obviously, I do not have this conversation with everyone. When a client requires confidentiality, I honor their request. But most of the time when people have had a great experience, they are willing to talk about it. These testimonials are a key component of the Just Sold mailers I send out and a vital part of building my geographic farm. I will talk a lot more about how to build a farm that will guarantee success in my next book. For now, please know that Just Solds are one of the very best ways to blast your name across a town or neighborhood. And if you can include a statement from someone who lived in that area that says, "Jordan Cohen was great to work with. He exceeded all our expectations," people not only will recognize your name, they will see you as someone who may exceed their expectations when it comes time to sell their home.

The Just Sold mailers are very different from the Just Listed brochures. For starters, they are much smaller, closer to a postcard than a brochure. Although the print quality is just as high as the Just Listed brochures, I only include one photo of the home. I also make no apologies about the fact that this mailer promotes me and my business, not the home. I not only include information about me and my brokerage, I also place my slogan in a prominent place: "Serious about selling? Interview Jordan Cohen . . . you'll be glad you did!" This is my way of asking everyone who receives the mailer to interview me to sell their home. More often than not, some will. Once again, I never ask for a listing in anything I mail or advertise. I simply ask for an interview. Let's be real. I doubt anyone will read a mailer or an ad in a newspaper that says, "List with Jordan Cohen," and then say, "We better list with this guy. He means business because he's *telling* us to list with him!"

I also include the selling price and other features of the home on the Just Sold mailers. Again, this is a great marketing tool to reach people who have kicked around the idea of possibly selling their home. I want them to see how much I was able to get for the Johnson house around the corner and have them say, "If he can get a price like that for *that* house, just think how much he can get for ours!"

Just Listed and Just Sold mailers work together not only in marketing your listings but in marketing you. Done right, they can boost your career, build your farm, and sell houses. On top of that, sellers love them. Taken together, the benefits far outweigh the cost to produce something high quality that makes a lasting impression. Remember, everything we send out is a reflection on us and the quality of work that we do. For me, investing in making a great first impression is money well spent.

9

PUTTING THE *AGENT* IN REAL ESTATE AGENT

When I first started thinking about writing this book, I knew I wanted to share my listing presentation, but I had one hesitation. Most trainers use scripts, but I never think of my presentation as a script to be memorized. That may seem odd given all the language I've given you to use, as well as the way in which I've set that language apart by using a different font. If it were anyone else's book, I'd say these all look like scripts to me. But I do not consider this to be a book of scripts because the word *script* implies something you recite verbatim, as if the language itself will somehow transfix those who hear it and will magically win the listing interview. Here's the sad reality: sellers will forget most of what you say before you even get up from the table and leave their house, but they will remember how we say it. Excitement and *confidence* are contagious. When sellers hear the passion in our voices and feel the confidence exuding from us, they catch it. They may not remember all the details of our marketing plans, but they will not forget our enthusiasm for the job of selling their home.

Show, Don't Tell

Enthusiasm and confidence describe the core of who we are as real estate *agents*. Remember, our job is very much like what a sports/entertainment agent does for their clients. We are the agents, and houses are our stars. Any agent who takes a half-hearted approach to finding their client their next gig or endorsement deal won't be in the business very long. Effective agents aggressively promote their stars with enthusiasm. They believe in their clients, and they are out there every day, doing their best to get sponsors and studios and teams to believe in them, too. Again, we are agents and our listings are our stars. Most sellers never make this connection, which is why we need to do it for them. Let me tell you, when we do, sellers love it. I say it like this:

> "After I send out the brochures, I will follow up with phone calls to all the homeowners in your area for whom I have their contact information. Let me tell you why. I've sold a lot of homes to actors and athletes, and one of the things I've learned from them is that their agents don't sit back and wait for deals to come to them. An actor's agent works the phones, calling studios, pushing their client for that next big part. A great athlete's agent gets out there and finds off-field promotions for their clients. They don't wait for Subway to call or for Nike to come around with a shoe deal. The best agents are on the phone every day, promoting their client.

"I am a real estate *agent*. Just like an agent in the world of entertainment, I will work the phones, calling not just others in the business who may have a client who is looking for a home exactly like yours but also my past clients and other people in my sphere of influence that I think may be ready to make a move and who would be interested in your house. I don't sit back and wait for potential buyers; I get out there and find them. I'm an agent and your house is my star. I'm going to do everything I can to put your home out there and promote it until we find that buyer who is willing to pay your price or more."

Sellers love the sports/entertainment agent analogy. Every seller who follows sports has read about the incredible deals agents land for star athletes. When we tell them that's the approach we will take with their home, sellers immediately get it. They can picture it in their mind. I see it all the time. The day before I started working on the marketing section of this book, I went out on a listing interview. I did my usual presentation, always tailoring my words to this specific seller and her home. When I got to the marketing part of my presentation, I talked about photos and social media and print ads and the mailers I planned to send out. Then I added an explanation of how I am an agent, like an athlete's or actor's agent, and her house is my star. "I'm going to work the phones to promote your home to as many people as I can," I said.

At the end of the interview, I wrapped up by saying, "I want you to be as confident in me as I am in myself that I am the agent who will truly be able to sell your home for the most amount of money. I know I have given you a lot of information to digest."

The seller then said, "Yes, you have, but you know, what really resonated with me was the idea that you are going to pick up the phone and call people to promote my house. Too many of the agents I've talked to seem to rely on sticking a home on the MLS and the internet. But you sound like you're really aggressive. I like that analogy. You're an agent and my house is your star."

"I appreciate you saying that," I replied, "because that's exactly the approach I take. You are not hiring me to list your house. You are hiring me to sell it. I only get paid when your house sells, which is why I have to be aggressive to find that buyer who will pay your price or more."

I won the listing, and I sold the house, all thanks to the most basic, easiest, and absolutely the cheapest tool in my marketing toolbox. Working the phones like an athlete's agent trying to get their client a shoe deal literally doesn't cost a dime beyond my monthly phone bill, but that's the one that struck a chord with this very wealthy seller. I find she is not alone. There is still a large element of people out there who love old-school hustle. And nothing is more old-school hustle than working the phones like Jerry Maguire, especially when our clients know that in the end we are going to "show them the money!"

Now here's the real question: Would I have won the listing without using the sports agent analogy? If I had told the seller I planned to follow up the Just Listed mailers with phone calls and nothing else, would that still have been the point that convinced her to list with me rather than another agent? I like to think that the rest of my presentation was so strong that I would have won the listing, but that sort of misses the point. When we sit down at a breakfast table with potential sellers for a listing interview, we are selling ourselves and our skill set. The seller doesn't know or fully appreciate what we bring to the table unless we can explain it to them in a way they can easily grasp.

While writing this book I learned that writers have a mantra of their own: Show, don't tell. That simply means that all of us get overwhelmed when bombarded with information. But we remember good stories and word pictures. That's what makes the sports agent analogy so effective. It communicates beyond words. Every seller has seen Steph Curry selling Subway sandwiches and Samuel L. Jackson asking us what's in our wallets in credit card commercials. Connecting those commercials to the way we will promote their house sticks in their minds. Sellers will forget most of what we say before we even finish our listing presentation, but they will remember pictures we draw for them. And that picture in their mind may well be the difference between winning and losing that listing interview!

And the Best Part Is It Doesn't Cost Anything Extra!

Up to this point, most of the marketing tools we've explored have violated the old real estate maxim that says, Don't spend money. Please keep in mind that there are ways to use these tools in an economic manner. I know this from firsthand experience because I had to make every dime count when I first started since I didn't have many dimes to begin with. We don't spend, we invest, and investing means putting our money to work in strategic ways. By now, though, many of you may well wonder when that strategic spending will come to an end. If that's you, I have good news. The last tool I pull out of the toolbox during my listing presentation doesn't cost anything but time. One of the tools I use the most doesn't cost a dime beyond your monthly phone bill. And this tool works, and it wins listing interviews. This tool shows the seller that we plan to hit the ground running. I explain it to sellers like this:

"Mr. Seller, I've talked to you about all the different tools I will use to promote your home to as many potential, qualified buyers as possible. And I have one more that will let us hit the ground running. The day before your listing goes live, I will do a massive prelaunch blast through email and social media. I will put together an amazing Coming Soon email featuring a few of the best photos of your home that will go out to thousands of real estate agents and to my past clients and to anyone and everyone I know that will want to see your house. Twenty-four hours before your house hits the MLS, this email will land in thousands of inboxes.

"At the same time, I will do my first post about your home on Instagram. Think of this as a trailer that studios do for upcoming feature films. I'm going to give my followers a slide show of epic photos and key amenities along with the words 'Coming Soon!' Then, when your home hits the MLS and all the real estate sites on the internet, people are looking for it. They can't wait to see it, and they'll want to see more than a few photos online. They'll call to schedule a time to come see your home, and that's the point of every marketing tool I will use. All of them are designed to get potential qualified buyers excited enough about your home to come see it with me in person. And that's where I can use my skills as a salesman to close the deal with one of them. We're looking for that one buyer, or better yet, multiple buyers, who will pay your price or more."

I say all of this with confidence, conviction, and passion. I know the prelaunch blast works, just as I have full confidence in every part of my marketing plan. But it is not enough for me to feel this way. Through every step of the marketing section of my presentation, we need to convey enthusiasm and explain how each step works.

Now, do I always use all the marketing tools I have laid out to the seller? No. I always hire a photographer for epic pictures of the home. And I always post my listings on my personal MLS, that is, my Instagram page. I also do the prelaunch email and social media blast. Many times this is enough. A listing will sell so quickly that there is no time to do print or mailers for that particular listing. But I still use those tools on enough of my listings that they still work to build my brand and establish or expand my geographical farm. I am not being disingenuous with the seller when I talk about using all of these tools. I've yet to have a seller be upset that their home sold so fast that I did not have time to put an ad for it in *Homes & Land*.

I also do not always mention every one of these tools in my listing presentation. Remember, I cater my presentation to the seller. I try to get a sense from them which tool in my toolbox will resonate with them, and I go straight to it.

Like I wrote previously, I do not believe my list of tools to be exhaustive. You may have marketing techniques and strategies that work for you that I've never thought about, which is great. I do not pretend to know everything there is about winning a listing interview. Use what works for you. The only piece of advice I offer is, when you bring that tool out of your marketing toolbox, talk about it with confidence and passion, and explain why this tool is so effective. We must never take anything for granted when it comes to selling ourselves. I find it is better to overexplain than to assume the seller gets it and end up losing that listing.

My listing presentation does not end with the marketing section. In fact, I'm just getting started. Like I tell sellers, the whole point behind our marketing strategy is to get a buyer to come see the home. Only then can we get down to why we are in this business to begin with: showing the home and closing the sale!

10

THE PREGAME

There's an old real estate saying out there—one that old agents and trainers often cite right before telling us that we don't need to spend money to promote our listings—that says if you price a house right, buyers will automatically find you. The last six chapters shot down that idea. But the old saying doesn't stop there. If buyers are going to come find you, that implies the house will sell itself. I don't need six chapters to shoot that one down. Unless houses are priced below value, houses don't sell themselves. We sell them. We are salespeople. We can strongly push one house over another. We can overcome objections and give our opinions. If we are good at our jobs, we can create urgency and sell a house for the highest possible price and the best terms. That's why we promote them as hard as we do. We cast a wide net to bring in as many qualified buyers as possible to come see the listing in person. Then, once we get them in the house, we switch from promoter to salesperson and close the deal.

There's another old saying that says the secret to sales is to give the people what they want. I happen to agree with that one, with a slight modification. When it comes to selling houses, the key is to *show* buyers what they want, and the only way to know what they want is to prescreen them before they ever arrive for that first showing. A lot of us have been preconditioned to think that pre-screening buyers consists of little more than having them prequalify for a mortgage. After all, there's no point in showing someone a house they cannot afford. But price is only one factor in finding the right home. Buyers have a long list of what they hope to find in a new home, a list that constantly evolves with the more houses they see. Buyer's agents know this all too well.

But this chapter is not for buyer's agents. It's for listing agents, and as listing agents it should be our goal to learn as much as we can about every potential buyer whether they are our clients or not. We've already explored in depth how we plan to promote the house across a wide variety of media. Now it is time to narrow the conversation down to how we plan to sell it, beginning with a screening process that will transform the way you show a house while also convincing sellers that you are the salesperson they must have to get top dollar out of their home. Anyone can sell below market. Some can sell for fair market. But, as we all know, most sellers want "their price" or more. Usually this can be slightly above market. If every house were priced right, then every house would sell immediately. Agree? When we prescreen buyers the right way, we give ourselves the best shot to take advantage of every showing and sell!

Screening Buyers Beyond Prequalification

I explain my screening process to sellers in my listing presentation like this:

"I am not going to schedule a showing the moment someone calls about your house. I first screen every buyer. I do this, first of all, to make sure they are actually serious about buying a home and are financially able to do so. I do not want to disrupt your lives and have you scramble around to get everything ready for a showing just to find out the 'buyer' is a couple looking to get ideas on how to remodel their kitchen or are looking at houses because it's cheaper than going to the movies. Surprisingly, this often happens. A percentage of my viewing requests are for many reasons other than to actually purchase a house. I'm very diligent in my efforts to ensure that every showing is with a vetted and qualified buyer looking to buy now. I also ask what they do for a living and where they are moving from. Because yours is a luxury home, I will most likely be able to google buyers to see if they are legit. If not, I insist on proof of funds before showing them your home."

Obviously, you will modify the above to fit the market where you work. If you work in a KeySafe market, rather than telling the seller you will insist on proof of funds, you will tell the seller that you will insist on a prequalification letter from a mortgage company before scheduling a showing. *Sellers love this.* I have never had a seller tell me, "What? You're going to insist potential buyers are actually qualified to buy my home before you show it? No, no, no. I want you to bring in anyone and everyone who wants to see it. I love total strangers going through my house and taking inventory of all my stuff."

I will once again say:

"Again, I don't want to waste your time or mine on a showing for someone who is not able to buy either now or in the future.

"But the screening I do is not primarily about eliminating fake buyers or nosy neighbors. All of the marketing plans we discussed are designed to get as many qualified buyers as possible interested in your home. The more important reason I ask screening questions is to help me know as much as possible about each person who will come to see it so that I can point out and emphasize the features that I already know in advance they are looking for. This also enables me to do my best to schedule a showing at the right time of day. If the potential buyers currently live and work in the city but want to move here, I will do my best to schedule showings early in the day or on weekends. Nothing is worse than scheduling a showing on a Friday at four o'clock, knowing the buyers will get crushed in traffic on their way. I've seen buyers rethink their desire to move based on traffic alone."

Trust me. Scheduling showings around traffic will score points for you not only in Los Angeles but in any city. These are the little details most sellers never consider, but when we bring it up, sellers see it as genius. It's also a little insight most agents may not consider. I learned this the hard way. My good friend Josh Altman* called me one day about one of my listings. He said, "Hey man, I just got off the phone with one of my big-time celeb clients. He wants to see your $85 million listing in North Ranch."

"Wow. That is fantastic. When does he want to see it?" I asked. Due to confidentiality, I cannot say who the client was, but trust me, he is an A-lister.

"Friday at four."

---

* In a later chapter I tell the story of how Josh and I first met. It's hilarious, at least it is to me. I still rib Josh about it all these years later.

"Josh, I know who your client is, and he lives in Beverly Hills. The house is up in Westlake. Do you have any idea what the traffic is going to be like when he drives back on a Friday evening? It will be a wasted showing. Can you get him out here earlier in the day?"

"No," Josh said, "It's the only time he can come up to see it, and we have to work around his schedule. Don't worry. It'll work out. He will love it."

Josh and his client arrived right on time in separate cars. Traffic was light when they drove up. The first thing his client said when he got out of the car was, "Only forty-five minutes from the city? That was easy." It was a good start that only got better as I started the tour of the twenty-five-thousand-square-foot main house. Josh's client was an artist, with an artist's eye for detail. He took his time, examining every room with a smile that grew larger the more of the home I showed him. He didn't have to say a word for me to know how much he loved everything about the house. Once we finished touring the main house, we climbed into golf carts to tour the rest of the twenty-acre estate. Josh's client loved the two pools and pool houses and Vegas-quality spa. He loved the multiple guest houses, one of which was eleven thousand square feet. By the time we got to the replica of the Monet garden I knew he didn't have to see anything else. This was the house. The five-acre organic farm and fully stocked fishing lake were just more icing on the cake.

By the time we finished, the three of us shook hands. The client thanked me for showing him the house. "I love it," he said with a big smile. Then he added, "It doesn't matter, but if you could get me the operating expenses for the estate from the sellers, I would appreciate it. Like I said, I love the place, so the expenses don't matter. I'm just curious."

"You bet," I said. "I'll call the business manager and get those for you as quick as I can."

Josh and I gave each other a little grin of satisfaction. We both knew this deal was a lock.

As soon as the two of them got in their cars and drove away, I called the business manager to start the process of running down all the numbers for Josh's client. An hour and a half later my phone rang. It was Josh. I answered with excitement, hoping to hear an offer was on its way. But Josh's tone of voice when he said hello told me I was about to hear bad news.

"Don't worry about getting that information for me," Josh said.

"Uh-oh. What happened?"

"He just called me from his car. He's not even close to his house yet. Traffic on the 101 is nuts. He hasn't even made it to the 405 exchange yet. He told me he loved the house, but he can't see making this drive back and forth to the city every day."

All I could do was shake my head. I knew the 101 is basically a parking lot every evening, and it's even worse on a Friday night. I could not help thinking that if we had scheduled the showing for eleven in the morning, Josh would have made a very different phone call. That's why I always ask where people work. I'm not trying to be nosy or figure out if they make as much money as they claim. It's all about eliminating obstacles with something as simple as knowing the right time of day to schedule your showings. When you explain this to sellers during your listing presentation, you automatically separate yourself from the pack.

Digging Deeper

Eliminating fake buyers and knowing the key times to set up showings is only one part of the equation. The next chapter focuses on how to show the house (*Spoiler alert*: it is best to show our listings ourselves). Before we are ready to show a specific buyer a home, we want to learn as much as we can about them. I look at it as being very much like what my good friend and three-time defensive player of the year and Los Angeles Rams superstar Aaron Donald does before every game. He spends hours watching film of every upcoming opponent. Aaron told me he does it to learn everything he can about his competition, their tendencies, and their movements. He's looking for that edge he can exploit in the game. That's part of what makes him the best player in football. My screening process has the same purpose. I want to be prepared and to know exactly what buyers are looking for in a house so that I can show it to them. I explain this to sellers like this. It is just one more way to demonstrate to the sellers our sales and marketing expertise:

> "Screening buyers is my way to learn as much as I can about them, and how your home fits into what they are looking for in a house. I ask a little about them and why your home appeals to them. I make note of all of their answers so that I can come back to them during the tour and make sure they remember them. I am a great real estate salesman."

Stress the word *salesman*. Don't be afraid to say this. Sellers appreciate confidence.

> "I know how to connect with buyers and help them see how your house is the perfect fit for them. I also know that sometimes you have to remind people why they are here. When I know in advance they are looking for the open-concept kitchen and family room that you have, I want to stress it on our tour. Again, screening buyers is all about giving me an edge on how to skillfully show your house to produce results. That's how we will get your price or more."

This whole process of screening buyers always resonates with sellers. Most value their privacy. They appreciate it when they learn that we value it as well. Sellers also do not want to upend their lives to make time for a showing to any "buyer" who isn't serious. They expect us to find qualified buyers, and I find they like hearing how we plan to do that.

The Best Laid Plans

Even with all our efforts to prescreen buyers and guarantee a great showing, sometimes it's the sellers who throw a wrench in our plans. Several years ago I had a listing in North Ranch that definitely fell into the "fixer" category. I arrived five minutes before the buyers and their agent. I rushed around and turned on as many lights as I could, including the primary bedroom and the guest rooms. The house was a mess. It was obvious the sellers had forgotten about the showing even though I reminded them the day before, but I couldn't do anything about that now. The doorbell rang and I hustled over to the door to greet the buyers and their agent. As soon as they walked into the house their facial expressions went from happy to shocked. Shit was everywhere and the house was a wreck. The buyers immediately asked, "Did these folks know we were coming?"

"Yes, they did," I said.

"Hmmm, that's surprising. I can't believe anyone would show a house in this condition."

"I know it's a mess, but the bones of this home are fantastic, and the price is fair and reasonable." I hoped they could see beyond the mess, but stepping into the primary bedroom threw them over the edge. We could hardly see the floors. Dirty dishes were stacked on the nightstands. The bed was a disheveled mess. "Oh my goodness," the buyers said, "this is disgusting. How can anyone live like this? This room is a pigsty!" It didn't take long for the potential buyers to see all they needed to see. I wrapped up the tour, but I knew no offer was going to be coming.

I turned off all the lights and left the house. About ten seconds later, my cell phone rang. It was the seller. She was obviously embarrassed. "I'm sorry I forgot about the showing," she apologized. "I'm actually home right now."

My heart sank at what I knew was coming next.

"I didn't just forget about the showing. I also overslept. I woke up when I heard the people come into the house. I didn't even have time to get up and get dressed, so I pulled the covers and bedspread over my head, stacked my pillows, and prayed you didn't notice I was under there."

I went numb. Not only was she home, she was in the primary bedroom the whole time! I knew exactly what was said in that room, and she had heard it all.

"I am mortified they saw my house like this."

I told her not to worry and assured her we would have better luck next time.

To this day, not only do I remind sellers both the day before but also the morning of every showing. I also arrive early enough to double-check that the home is ready for a showing. I also double-check to make sure no one is hiding under the covers. Sometimes you have to screen for everything.

11

IT'S SHOWTIME!

Years ago I attended a real estate retreat led by an iconic trainer. In one session, he introduced a panel of six of the top agents that followed his system. When he introduced the panel, one guy in particular grabbed my attention. Many real estate agents in Southern California, including me, held this guy in awe. He drove a Rolls-Royce when no one in real estate drove a Rolls. With his fancy, tailored suits and shiny shoes, he attracted an audience without saying a word.

But what really set him apart, what made him a real estate rock star, came out in the trainer's introduction: "This is _____ and he sells three hundred houses every year!" *Three hundred homes a year!* He was more than a rock star. That kind of production made him a real estate god! What most people in the room did not know was that this real estate god was not a member of the Multiple Listing Service, so we all had to take his word for his sales figures. The Rolls-Royce made him a lot easier to believe.

"And do you know how he sells three hundred houses a year? It's all about prospecting. _____ knocks on hundreds of doors a day. And the minute he gets a listing, he passes it along to his assistants and coordinators and never talks to those people again. His assistants take it from there because all his time is spent on prospecting. He has more doors to knock on, more listings to win. And that, ladies and gentlemen, is how you dominate a market!"

Everyone in the room, me included, sat there mesmerized. After the session, the real estate god came out into the foyer and into the presence of mere mortal agents like me. A dozen or so of us gathered around him like he was royalty. I glanced around at the looks in the agents' eyes, and you would have thought they were standing next to Elvis Presley.

Not too long after the seminar, my town was devastated by the 1994 Northridge earthquake. Like so many others, I was able to purchase damaged homes at a significant discount, fix them up, and sell them, aka, flipping. My first flip house was not expensive. I bought it for $50,000, invested another $15,000 in paint, carpet, and repairs and listed it for $99,000. I quickly received multiple offers, including one from the Real Estate Rock Star himself. *Holy crap*, I thought to myself. *This isn't just a chance to sell a house and pocket twenty thousand in profit, this is my chance to learn from the legend himself.* And boy did I learn from him.

I happily accepted the offer from him and signed the contracts. I thought I knew what to expect from the Real Estate Rock Star, but reality was a little different from my seminar experience. Throughout the entire escrow I received calls from him or his wife multiple times every day. Never once did I hear from an assistant or a coordinator. Like a lot of borrowers, their client was having trouble with their loan, which caused delays. The Real Estate Rock Star and his wife contacted me so often that it was obvious they were doing a lot of hand-holding as the buyer's agent. I found this more than a little strange, especially since this was the man who claimed to leave all the grunt work to his assistants.

After we finally closed the deal, I asked the Real Estate Rock Star's wife about something that had bothered me for some time. "I just went to a real estate seminar where your husband was a panelist," I said.

She started giggling, as if she knew what was coming next.

"As you know," I continued, "in the eyes of every agent in that grand ballroom, he's a legend, but he said he never speaks to his clients or the other agent once he gets a listing or once he gets a deal in escrow as a buyer's representative. That's the job of his coordinators and staff. Now, don't get me wrong. The two of you have been great to work with. You do what we all do in this business. In fact, you were very thorough and nice, but that's not what I expected when I accepted your client's offer."

She shook her head and said with a big smile, "Don't believe everything you see and hear from everyone you meet at those seminars. It's all about 'the Show.'"

Needless to say, I never went to another sales seminar again. Ever! It was at that very moment that I decided to do my best to create my own language and my own systems that work for me, but that's not the point of this story. When the Real Estate Rock Star said he spent all his time prospecting and left all the dirty work to his assistants, everyone in the audience applauded wildly. I guess we all wanted to believe what he was saying was true. We wanted to believe he had cracked the secret code of making money in real estate without having to deal with people directly.

But there is no code to crack. We may think we are in the real estate business, but in reality, we are in the people business. The people who hire us do not hire us to list their homes. They hire us to sell them. Early in my career I was told that if I set the price right, a house will basically sell itself. Perhaps that is true in a white-hot market, but in a normal market, houses never sell themselves. We do. Period. All the marketing we do to promote a listing is designed to bring potential buyers to the listing to see the house in person. And that's where we turn from marketers to salespeople. Showing the home with confidence is the key to selling the home, and *explaining* to sellers why our approach to showing their home is different from our competition is key to winning listings. We may be great marketers, but that's only half the job. As I tell sellers over and over, we never get paid when we list a house, only when we sell it. And to sell it, we have to show it effectively with all the hands-on people skills we have.

Nobody Does It Better

I move from the marketing section of my presentation to the showing section by saying:

> "Mr. Seller, all the marketing we just discussed is designed to do one thing: get qualified people to come see your home in person. They won't buy it until they come see it, and when they come to see it, I get to do what I love most, and that's selling houses. When it comes time to show your home to potential buyers, I will be here to give them a professional tour, answer their questions, overcome objections, and do my best to generate an offer. If for some reason I cannot be here for a showing, one of my assistants who has been properly trained and coached by me will be here in my place. But make no mistake about it. Showing your home is my number one priority. I schedule everything else I do around showings because that's what sellers pay me to do."

If you do not show your listings by appointment only and use key safes instead, tell the seller that you will use an electronic key safe and will personally call every agent after every showing and answer any questions they may have, explain the pricing, and address any objections they may have.

If the seller asks how I could possibly have time to show their home personally when I have so many other listings, I reply:

"That's a great question. But as Benjamin Franklin once said, if you want to get something done, ask a busy person. Showing my listings is always my top, day-to-day priority. I will always make the time to show your home and sell it. Remember, I only get compensated when I sell, so I will do whatever is necessary to give myself the best chance possible to sell your home. And that means showing my listings myself. I approach every one of my listings as its own separate business, and I am the CEO. Make no mistake. You are the chairman of the board. I work for you. But as the CEO of the business of selling your house, I will invest the time, money, and passion necessary to make it successful and profitable for us both. I assure you, nobody will work harder at selling your home than me."

It's okay to say this. People will understand this is a business and you are not there for shits and giggles. They will appreciate you saying how hard you will work in order to produce results.

"I want to tell you why it's critical for me or my showing assistant to show your home in person versus simply putting a lockbox on you front door so that buyers' agents can take their clients through on their own. The buyers' agent, who has never been in your home, will not know about the key features that set your home apart unless they just happen to stumble upon them. I don't want to leave that to chance. That's why I will be here to take buyers on the tour the right way."

This is where I go back to what the sellers said when they took me on a tour of their home. I recall specific features that mattered most to the sellers while also drawing on what I learn from buyers when I prescreen them. For example:

"I will point out the extra storage in the garage and all the other features that set your home apart. Remember when I talked about screening buyers and how I will ask about what is most important to them? I use their answers in my tour. I will remind buyers how this large grassy area in addition to the pool adds value and is obviously great for kids. By doing so, I will not only justify our price for your home but will also show the buyer that this is a great value. My goal isn't just to sell your home, but to sell it for the most money possible."

Reading the above, you can tell I prefer to show listings by appointment only, something I will return to later in the next chapter on open houses. But for many of you, showing by appointment only is not an option. If you live in an area where every listing uses a lockbox, you place yourself at a competitive disadvantage by not using one as well. But the same approach I describe above can still work. In those situations, I will say:

"I prefer showing homes myself, with showings by appointment only. In this area, however, where every listing has a lockbox, we will need to use one as well. But that does not mean we have to do the lockbox the same way as everyone else. I want to make sure the buyers' agents who bring clients to see your house do not miss all the beautiful features that made you fall in love with it. I want them to notice that extra storage space in the garage and the invisible dog fence you installed last year. That is why I will not put the lockbox on your front door but on the gate on the side of your home. Also, in the MLS, I will add a note that says, "Call listing agent prior to showing." I do this so that when agents call for the lockbox location and/or combination, I can sell *them* on your home and make sure they understand all the great features that set your home apart. I don't want them to go in blind. This will give them a much better chance to sell, not just show, your home."

The above is one of the primary ways we can set ourselves apart from other agents the sellers will interview. Showing our listings in person is probably the single most important thing we do. As the listing agent, we are the authority on this home. We know what sets it apart from similar homes. When questions come up about the price, and they always come up, we are there to justify it. Buyers may also want to know more about the neighborhood and the surrounding area. When the listing is in our geographic farms, we probably know more about the area than the buyer's agent. We can talk about the dog park on the next block or the coffee shop that just opened. Some of us may feel like we simply don't have the time to personally attend every showing of our listings or the resources to make sure an assistant is there in our place. The way I look at it, we can't afford not to be there.

Connections Made

When it comes to everything we do in this business, we must always think two or three steps ahead. Personally showing our listings is no exception. I've found this is another way to build our business and our careers. When we make a positive impression on the buyers, they may come back to us down the road when they are ready to list the property and the agent with whom they worked before has either retired, moved out of town, or is simply a buyer's agent. That's exactly how I connected with a client I now count as a very close friend, rock and roll icon Bret Michaels, who recently wrapped up a stadium tour.

I was already a huge fan before I received the call from the agent with whom Bret was working, asking about one of my listings in North Ranch. Even if I didn't already show all my own listings, I might have just to meet him. And he did not disappoint. He walked into the home in full-blown, rock-star mode with his faded jeans, sleeveless T-shirt, trademark bandana, and a Pittsburgh Pirates ballcap. I've worked with many pop and rock stars before and since meeting Bret. Some treated me like a peasant they could barely bring themselves to acknowledge. One or two made it clear I was never to gaze directly upon them, like they were some kind of goddess. Bret was exactly the opposite. Even though he's sold more than fifty million albums and is one of the wealthiest clients I have worked with, he is one of the most genuinely caring, nicest, and friendliest guys I've ever met. Five minutes after I met him, we were laughing like we'd known each other forever.

When it came to the house, Bret knew exactly what he was looking for. He asked great questions that made it clear he was much more real estate savvy than the average buyer. He was also a cash buyer, which meant he was ready to go. As an artist, he was looking for a place with great energy, good karma. By the time he made an offer, he toured the home three times. He brought his wife, Kristi, and his daughters, Raine and Jorja, a couple times as well. I met him at the property every time and walked with him through the entire process. His agent was also very nice and wonderful to work with.

A few years later, when Bret and his wife decided to sell their North Ranch home, he called me. The agent through whom he bought the home had since retired and moved out of state. Since then we've done several deals together, and he has made every deal for the buyer and himself good karma. More than that, he's become a good friend. In fact, he even jokes with me about letting me fulfill my inner rock-star dreams. He's promised that one day he'll let me play the bongos on stage. In Bret's autobiography his impressive lesson is to "Bet on Yourself." I couldn't agree more and who knows? That might just lead to my next career, Bret Michaels's bongo player.

Explaining how we plan to show a house is just one more tool in the toolbox that effectively wins listings. Explaining how we show a house is equally if not more important than how we market it. Sellers want to entrust the sale of their most valuable asset to the one they believe will take the best care of it. This is just one more place where our professionalism and salesmanship will trump listing a home with an old friend from college who does real estate as a side hustle. Remember, by the time we reach the end of the listing presentation, we want the seller to have as much confidence in us as we have in ourselves. By this point, that confidence should be growing, which we need as we move into the next phase of the listing presentation, setting the right price.

But before we move on to pricing, we need to address one of the classic tools for showing a home that many of us were taught we cannot live without: open houses. Whether you use them or not, the next chapter is for you.

12

OPEN HOUSES?

Any conversation about showing listings must include open houses, right? After all, most sellers expect them, at least that's what conventional wisdom says. Conventional wisdom also says that open houses are the best way to show a listing to the largest number of people at one time. It's a simple formula. List a home on Wednesday or Thursday. Schedule an open house for Saturday or Sunday. Collect multiple offers. Take the best one with the best terms to your client on Monday and change the listing status to "under contract" on Tuesday. If you follow this formula and it works for you, great. Keep doing what you are doing. Like I said earlier in the book, one of the keys in real estate is figuring out the process that works best for you and running with it. But for those of you looking for another way, keep reading.

Open Houses and Lead Generation

People often ask me how I built my business. Through my first seven years in real estate, I sat open houses *every* Saturday and

Sunday. My wife understood every single weekend was for open houses, not for ballgames or parties or getaways. Instead I spent every single Saturday and Sunday sitting in an empty house waiting for prospective buyers to walk through the door. And when they did, I said the exact same thing we all have been trained to say:

"Welcome. My name is Jordan. Here's a brochure. Let me tell you a little bit about the house before you take a look.

"Would you like a personal tour, or do you prefer to walk through the home on your own?

"Let me know if you have any questions.

"So what do you think? Any interest?

"How long have you been looking for a home?

"Do you have any feedback I can offer to the seller?

"Would you like to schedule a second, private showing?

"Are you looking for yourself or a friend or family?

"If this home doesn't work for you, can you tell me what features are important to you in your next home? I may have other options.

"Are you already working with another agent?

"May I show you other homes that may have more of the features you are looking for?"

We all ask these questions for the same reason: to land buyers. If this house doesn't work for them, and our first goal is always to sell the house we're sitting, we're ready to show them a dozen more. That's how we become buyers' agents. An open house is probably the best tool out there for building up your list of potential buyers. But, surprisingly, that's not the reason I devoted so much time to open houses.

Early on it dawned on me that all the questions I had been trained to ask at an open house were designed to either find a buyer for the current listing or to land a client as a buyer's agent. But my goal had always been to become primarily a listing agent. Therefore,

I had to ask myself, *Can I use open houses to land more listings?* I discovered I could, but to do so, I needed a different set of priorities. I adopted three distinct goals for every open house I sat. A word of warning to my clients who may be reading this book. This book is written first for real estate agents, which is why I am going to be completely transparent. My goals came in this order:

1. Sell the home I was sitting.

2. Land listing interviews.

3. Pick up buyers.

These goals required I start asking a new set of questions, beginning with, "Do you plan to sell your current home before you buy, or do you plan to buy and then sell?" I say this in a tone that sounded like I assumed they were already homeowners and they were out there looking at homes purely to upgrade or downsize. The responses I hoped to hear were either "sell then buy" or "buy then sell." Obviously, first-time buyers come through all open houses depending on the price of the listing, but I always asked the question with the assumption that they currently had a home to sell.

I always then asked, "Fantastic. I love to hear it. Are you planning on interviewing agents for the job of selling your house?"

The dream answer, the one we always hoped to hear, was, "Yes!" I immediately followed up with, "That's great news. I would love to be one of them."

Usually, however, I received one of two other responses. More often than not people said, "No, not yet," even if they intended to put their home on the market. Anonymity and not having to make any kind of immediate commitment to an agent they just met are part of the appeal of going to an open house. That's why people almost always said, "No, not yet."

Their evasiveness did not dissuade me. I said, "When do you plan to interview agents? Would it be okay if we stay in contact?" Depending on their answer, assuming they said, "We don't know," I would say, "I certainly do not mean to be pushy. Hopefully, when the time comes for you to interview agents, I can be one of them. I am confident that no one markets a home more aggressively than I do."

Aggressive is the key word that resonates and pops even with those who may not list their home for months. One more note: be prepared to deliver brief portions of your listing presentation during this conversation. I usually mentioned what I do differently from other real estate agents, including how I use social media or print ads. This is always brief. We do not want to overwhelm with information, especially when other people are coming in and out of the open house. Instead, we want to give just enough to capture their attention so that hopefully they will remember us when we contact them later either through text, email, or by phone.

Before this potential client left the open house, I always asked again, "I know you said you are not ready to interview agents at this time, but would you like me to come by to see your home and give you a quick value check? No obligation of course. I always have buyers who may be interested in a home like yours right now."

"Yes" and "not yet" are better than hearing "no" when asked if they will interview agents to list their home. When I heard this, I probed a little deeper. More often than not I heard the same response we all hear, "I've sort of promised my brother-in-law's best friend that we would go with him." When they said this, I smiled and went straight into the conversation I outlined in chapter 2 about how to land more listings.

For me, every person who entered my open houses was a potential listing. I always struck up conversations about the possibility of them selling. I made sure I had a presentation book and contracts in my car just in case they wanted me to see their home and interview immediately after the open house. The best line I said is, "As you know, the job of a real estate agent is to maximize the exposure of your home. Nobody casts a wider net than me. Please allow me twenty minutes to show you how I do it." I've said this line so many times, I should have had it trademarked.

For seven years I used open houses to get more listing interviews. And it worked. Before long the other agents in my office started asking how I got so many listings. Here I was, two or three years in the business and yet listing two or more homes a week spread out over the entire San Fernando Valley. Believe me, I did much more than use open houses to get listing interviews. I used creative and innovative lead generation tactics, out-of-the-box prospecting, and proven techniques to dominate a geographical farm. But open houses were a key part of my strategy. Every time I did one, I made it my goal to walk away with at least one new listing interview. When the open house was in my farm, the payoff was even sweeter. Not only did I land more interviews, but I also increased my influence in the area, which led to more listings and more sales, and up until fifteen years ago, more open houses. That is why I highly recommend every new agent set up open houses for their own listings, or volunteer to sit them for other agents. Every person who walks through the door of an open house presents three opportunities for you. You just have to be ready.

But all of this is not something a seller wants to hear during their listing interview with you. Sellers don't have three goals for an open house on their property. They only have one: sell their home. Therefore, the question for those of us who use open houses is how do we present them to sellers in a way that gives us an advantage over those who don't? Conversely, for those of us who prefer not to do open houses, and I am one of those at this point in my career, how do we explain our approach to a seller? Going in, many sellers expect us to hold open houses for their home. If they expect, or even demand them, how do we sell the idea that open houses not only don't work, but they can actually hurt our chances for a successful sale?

Love them or hate them, I have language for how to effectively present two completely different approaches.

For Those Who Do

By definition, an open house is a passive approach to selling a home. We put the date on the MLS, which then goes to the real estate websites. We may even do an email blast or an ad in the paper. The morning of the open we strategically place signs all over the neighborhood. Then we sit back and wait for potential buyers to show up. This is how most of us were trained to do open houses.

As I've written many times, sellers appreciate an aggressive approach to marketing and selling their home. They're looking for an agent who is going to get out there and expose their home to as many people as possible and then draw them in to personally tour their home. When I make the case for doing an open house, this is exactly the approach I take. I tell the sellers something along the lines of:

> "Ms. Seller, most of the real estate agents you will interview will tell you they want to hold an open house. They will tell you that this is the best way to show your home to the largest number of people in one day. I agree. An open house is a great way to show your home to a lot of people at the same time,

especially in a hot market like we have today. Our hope is always that by the end of the day we will receive at least one offer, or better yet, multiple offers.

"However, experience has taught me that if we do an open house the way people have been doing open houses for decades, the odds are extremely slim that anyone will walk through the door and buy it. I say this because the traditional approach to open houses is very passive. We put out signs and wait for something to happen.

"I take a far more aggressive approach. Of course, I announce the open house on the MLS, internet, and place signs everywhere I can. But I don't want to sit back and *hope* prospective buyers come along. A few days before the open house I plan to email a special invitation to everyone I included on my prelaunch email blast. This includes other real estate agents, past clients and brokers, not to mention my entire database of contacts. I will invite brokers to bring their clients to get a jump-start on the competition. Hopefully they will see firsthand the excitement my open houses generate.

"On top of that, I plan to go door to door within your neighborhood and personally invite your neighbors to your open house. Why would I do that? I have found that many times your neighbors have a friend or family member that they would like to see move into this neighborhood. Also, there is a good chance that some of your neighbors may be looking to downsize/upsize their homes, but because they love this area so much they haven't yet made a move. Your home may be exactly what they are looking for.

"I will invite as many people as I can to your open house because the more people we can get here, the more energy and excitement will build around your home. People come to open houses because it gives them a chance to see a home in a more relaxed and casual way. The vast majority of the people who show up will say they are just looking around to see what's out there, or they will say they are looking at the home for a friend. They will say this even if they are seriously considering buying your home. That's just human nature. But when they come here and see a lot of people, it creates a sense of urgency. The casual shopper knows they have to become a serious buyer really quickly. That sense of urgency often leads to multiple offers.

"Now I want you to fully understand what you are committing to when you agree to hold an open house. It is a public event. Anyone can come. And yes, we will have some neighbors walk through just because they're nosy. We will also have a certain number of people who have seen the beautiful photos of your kitchen backsplash online and want to see it in person because they are thinking about doing the same thing in their house. These people always come. But they can work to our advantage because they help build the crowd that builds the sense of urgency that in turn will cause those who are truly interested in your home to make an offer.

"Also, I want to assure you that I will be here to sit your open house or there will be an experienced, well-trained agent in my place. One of us will be here to give personalized tours, answer questions, overcome objections, and work to sell your home. Our goal with all of our marketing is to make as many people as possible aware of your home. On the day of the open house, I want to draw those people in and sell your home!"

In a hot market, the above may seem like overkill. When the housing inventory is low, buyers are constantly on the hunt for an open house. They don't need email invitations. All you have to do is post the day and time on Zillow, and they'll be lined up around the block before you can unlock the front door. At least that's how it feels in those parts of the country with housing shortages.

But whether the market is hot or cold, the way we talk about an open house in our listing presentation is geared toward the seller. Our goal is not just to tell them our strategy for showing their home but to convince them that our approach is better than anyone else they may interview. The previous language is designed to win listings. Does that mean all of this language is nothing but a load of BS to use to blow away the seller? Not at all. In those rare occasions when I hold open houses for a client who insists upon them, I do everything I outlined previously, including sitting the open myself. Sellers appreciate that personal touch. After all, they are hiring you to be the one to sell their home, not one of your assistants.

For Those Who Don't

After reading all my reasons why open houses work along with the way in which I used them to build my career, you may wonder why I stopped. To be honest, I truly feel showing my listings by appointment only is a much more effective way to sell houses. That may sound a little counterintuitive, especially since we all compete with agents who make open houses the centerpiece of their sales strategy. In the years since I stopped doing open houses, however, I have discovered that most sellers are relieved to hear I don't want to do one. As for competing against agents who make open houses sound like the slam dunk way to sell a house, I feel otherwise. I think not using open houses actually gives me an advantage. I explain it to sellers like this:

> "Mr. Seller, I know other agents you may interview will tell
> you they plan to hold open houses every weekend. They make

it sound like it is the single greatest way to attract buyers to your home. However, I do not do open houses because there are better ways of showing your home and more productive ways to find the buyer who is willing to pay your price or more. In fact, I strongly believe open houses may hurt our chances to sell to that perfect buyer who will pay top dollar. I am an aggressive real estate agent. All of my marketing tools are designed to pull in prospective buyers. Open houses, however, are a very passive approach. I could schedule one and end up sitting in your home for four hours on a Saturday and not have anyone show up other than real estate groupies who tour open houses every weekend because it is cheaper than going to the movies. I would much rather be available to show your home to serious buyers who deserve a private showing so that they can tour your home the right way.

"Speaking of serious buyers, I believe an open house actually limits my ability to sell your home. Let me tell you why. Open houses are public events with signs in your yard and notices on Zillow and other online realty sites. Many times a serious buyer will see the notice and come to the open house. They believe it is the easiest way to tour the house at their leisure without hearing a sales pitch from the listing agent.

"The problem is, I often find I get stuck answering questions about kitchen backsplashes from those touring open houses in search of redecorating ideas or cornered by a mortgage broker pitching me his latest products. This can and will prevent me from having a real conversation with a serious buyer. As a result, that buyer misses a lot of the features that make your home the perfect fit for them. Worse yet, they hear other people talking about how they think the second bedroom is too small, and that makes our real buyer question it as well.

"The point is, the odds are very good that we will miss out on a sale because a potential buyer did not get the proper tour of your home with me that they deserve. All the benefits of me personally showing your home are then lost. Not only do I lose the chance to point out the best features of your home, I also miss out on the opportunity to answer their questions and address any concerns they may have. Basically, I don't get to do what you have hired me to do.

"We also lose the ability to screen buyers. I do my best to only schedule showings with those seriously looking to buy a home and to find out everything I can about them for the reasons I explained earlier. An open house is a free-for-all. Anyone can come and they do.

"Now, I know some real estate agents will come in here and push for an open house because an open house is one of the best tools we have for picking up prospective buyers as clients. We are all trained to think that way. We're told to hold as many open houses as we can so that we can meet all your neighbors and perhaps pick them up as clients now or down the road. But you are not hiring me to hold an event that will build my business. You hire me to sell your home. And that's what I plan to do. Frankly, I am not interested in meeting your neighbors and getting stuck answering questions about the paint colors you chose. I would rather use that time to show your home to serious buyers, personally, one at a time."

When I go up against other agents whose entire strategy is built around holding open houses, I win nearly every time. The idea that every seller wants to have an open house is a myth. Most people guard their privacy. They tell me how they did not want a parade of strangers trekking through their home. Throw in the fact that sometimes thieves use open houses to case a place, and you can see why my anti–open house language is welcomed by sellers.

The Choice Is Up to You

Whether you use open houses or not, the choice really comes down to which approach works for you. Even though I choose not to do them, I will occasionally go out on a listing interview and find a seller who is dead set on having one. When that happens, I will reluctantly do one. After all, we are in the service business. Sometimes we have to do things we do not want to do just to please our clients even when what they are asking for is unproductive. At this stage of the game, if sitting an open house is the make-or-break moment to win the listing, we all have a business decision to make.

13

NAVIGATING THE TURBULENT WATERS OF PRICING

The year was 1992 but it could just as well have been 2022. I went on a listing interview for a tract house in Granada Hills in the San Fernando Valley. I started off then like I do now, by establishing credibility. Since I didn't yet have a lot of experience, I explained how I was trained in all the latest techniques and had a strong office full of mentors and support. The seller stayed with me. I presented my marketing strategy, starting with the photographs I planned to take along with the Just Listed mailers and print ads and working the phones. Then I walked the seller through how I planned to show the home, and in those days I even offered to hold the home open every weekend. The interview could not have been going better. I sensed the seller was about to pull the trigger and say, "Jordan, let's do this!"

And then we started talking about price.

"Mr. Johnson," I said, "the surrounding market has been fairly active, which gives us a pretty good idea of where we should come in with the price of your home. An exact model match just sold for $185,000 and another two blocks over sold for $187,500. Although your house is directly under a freeway overpass, which, as I'm sure you know, could affect value, I believe we can still ask $189,000."

The seller looked like he had seen a ghost. His eyes got wide, and he literally appeared to shake with nerves. With a high-pitched voice, he said, "Jordan, I think you are way off in your evaluation."

I could tell by his reaction he did not mean *way off* as too high. "What price do you have in mind?" I asked.

He replied with a straight face, albeit in a timid fashion: "We think it's worth $240,000."

Okay, I thought, *I've got a seller here who is nuts.* But I really wanted this listing. I'd walked away from too many houses with sellers who wanted insane prices only to see them come on the market with another agent at the price I recommended. I did not want to let that happen again. So I asked, "Mr. Johnson, please help me understand why your house is worth more than $50,000, basically 25 percent, than the two exact model matches that closed within the past month? Please keep in mind that neither were directly under the 118 overpass."

Again, with panic in his voice, he said, "I have things those other houses don't have."

We'd already been on a tour of the property. I think if he had a built-in treasure chest full of pirates' jewels or a hidden floor safe that included five Rolexes, I would have noticed them. I then asked with a slight hint of sarcasm, "Mr. Johnson. That's great news. I'm not sure what I could have missed that could fetch such a price jump, but I'm excited to hear it. Once again, my goal is to sell your home for the very highest price. So please tell me what exciting things you have that the two others didn't."

Again, he looked a little nervous as he said with a hint of indignation in his voice, "Well, I seriously doubt those other houses are decorated as beautifully as mine. And, uh, you know, I've made a lot of upgrades. I, uh"—he paused for just a moment—"I even installed brand-new oak toilet seats and ceiling fans!"

It's a good thing I'm a pretty good poker player and could keep a straight face. My first thought was, *Did he really just say oak toilet seats and ceiling fans?* I wondered if there was a hidden camera. I could not believe what I just heard.

I paused for a moment, trying to think of exactly the right thing to say. I had three choices. First, I could run for the door, thinking this loon could snap at any moment. Second, I could give in and list the house for $240,000 and deal with the embarrassment from my friends in the office and my colleagues all laughing at me during the brokers' caravan. Not to mention wasting time and money in marketing. Or, third, I could try to reel this seller back into reality in a way that would neither insult nor embarrass him.

"Mr. Johnson," I said, "I appreciate what you're saying. When you took me on the tour of your home I noticed those ceiling fans, and they look great. And the oak toilet seats, that's the kind of touch that may make some buyers choose yours over the others for sale. But the problem is, given the comps in your area, your home will not appraise for $240,000, which means any deal for that amount will never close."

I paused for a moment to let that news sink in. I then added, "I know you are probably thinking we can target cash buyers and not worry about the mortgage companies' appraisals." I wanted to then say that anyone with cash would certainly run to the closest exit the second they saw those hideous oak toilet seats. Instead I continued, "I'd love to find a cash buyer. They make the entire process of selling your home much easier. The problem, though, is cash buyers are deal buyers, and it is impossible to justify your home as a deal at $240,000. I'm sure you can understand that."

After a reasonable and logical debate, Mr. Johnson came around. He needed to sell and was grasping for straws at $240,000. Sometimes the seller needs some sensitivity and hand-holding to come to reality. We listed his home for $189,000 and accepted an offer of $180,000 a few weeks later, which was exactly what I thought the home would bring.

The Final Step

This conversation took place more than thirty years ago, but I still have variations of it today. We all do. We run into it with tract homes where a seller's home is worth $180,000 but they want $240,000. It happens with ultraluxury homes where a seller's home is worth four million, but they want to list it for six. And it happens with something in between with a house that should bring $350,000 but the seller wants $425,000 because the Zestimate put it between $340,000 and $390,000. It happens because, to us, pricing a home is about running numbers. But not for the seller. Not all sellers can separate their emotions from logic. They take great pride in things that may not add value to the home, but it does to them, even if that value comes in the form of memories. Not all sellers understand market dynamics. They have a hard time understanding how the $100,000 they put into their new kitchen does not necessarily add $100,000 in value, especially in a neighborhood where the average house sells for under three hundred thousand.

That is why pricing comes at the end of my listing presentation rather than at the beginning. Before we talk numbers, we want the

NAVIGATING THE TURBULENT WATERS OF PRICING   151

seller to understand we are professionals with a high level of both sales and marketing expertise. The presentation begins establishing credibility, but the entire presentation builds a stronger and stronger case for it throughout. By the time we get to pricing, the seller should believe they can fully trust our judgment. They should know we want to sell their home as badly as they do, and we are willing to back up our words with a significant investment to get it sold. If we've done our job, they're already thinking they not only want us to list their home, they need us to do it if they are going to get anywhere close to their price or more.

After establishing all of this, the seller is much more likely to listen when we begin the discussion of price. I always start by saying:

> "Now, Mr. Seller, let's talk about price. Hopefully my valuation is even higher than yours. Nothing would make me happier. Please share what price point you're thinking."

Half the time the seller will respond with something like, "Well, I won't sell my home for less than . . ." and they throw out a number. I always appreciate it when sellers do this because at least that gives me a starting point. But the other half of the time the seller will go fishing and say, "You are the expert. You tell me." Honestly, I don't blame them for that response. If I were in their shoes, I would say the same thing.

From this point on, my presentation to sellers about pricing probably looks very much like every other agent's. I talk about comps because we all have to talk about comps. Comps and appraisal value go hand in hand. But comps alone are not enough. When the market is in flux, either shooting up or tumbling down, what a house sold for six months ago has little bearing on what the same house will sell for today.

I've also found sellers do not want to hear us go on and on about comps. The three biggest complaints I get from sellers when I ask them why they listed with me rather than the competition are: other agents talk only about themselves and all the houses they've sold; other agents talk only about the company/brokerage for which they work; *and other agents talk only about comps.*

That's why, when it comes to comps, I give as many as I need to but no more than absolutely necessary. In fact, whenever possible, especially in my farm, which happens to be luxury estates, I say, "I don't need to talk about comps. I assume you already know about every public sale when it comes to luxury custom estates like yours. Every home is different and unique." The sellers with whom I work love it.

I then move to how we need to set the price right because our best chance to sell their home for the most amount of money is immediately after launch. Again, that's not original to me. We all know this. Even the nonagents reading this book know this. Anyone who has ever shopped for a house for more than a day always pays the most attention to the newest listings. The longer a house is on the market, the less attention it receives and the more likely the price will have to be dropped, or worse still, the listing will expire before the house actually sells.

Most sellers believe they should set the list price higher than what they expect to receive in order to give themselves room to negotiate with an interested buyer. Real Estate 101 says you are far more likely to miss buyers with a higher price. Buyers set price-based search parameters. Anyone looking for houses under $700,000 will go right past a house listed for $710,000. That is why all of us do our best to get that seller to list their home between $695,000 and $699,900. The lower number will produce more showings and multiple offers. In the right market, the seller may well get their price or more. I always tell sellers, "I can't guarantee I can sell your house for your price, but I can guarantee I give you the best chance because I will do everything I possibly can to make that happen. My marketing will expose the home to more buyers, and my sales skills and expertise will hopefully get one to pay it." Then I throw at the sellers what they always say to us. "It only takes one and it's my job to find that one and close them. Let's price it within reason and ride on the new listing momentum."

Finally, I explain why it is best to have the right price when we first list it rather than drop the price later if the house does not sell. Again, I did not think of this on my own. We all know that when buyers see a listing that's been on the market for a while drop its price, especially in a hot market, they start wondering what's wrong with it. In a normal market or one that is dropping, sellers risk losing money by having their home on the market too long. I always tell clients they can either get out in front of the train and price their home aggressively, sit on top of the train and ride it down, or get behind and hold on for dear life. Let's get in front of it from the beginning.

Here's another chance to overcome a common objection to a seller before they say it to us. We have all heard this one. "I'm not going to give my house away." So I will say it first. "If you want to give your house away, go with a discount agent who only wants to sell your home quickly and at any price. But if you really want maximum dollars, then you need someone like me with a proven track record and a game plan that yields results."

Steering a Seller to the Right Number

Every real estate agent is trained in what to say when it comes to pricing. The big question is how do we move a seller with an inflated number in their head back to the realities of the market? For me, the secret sauce is everything I say in the listing presentation leading up to pricing. If I lead with price, the seller has no good reason to listen to me. To them, I am nothing more than a salesman looking to make a quick sale, which means giving a home a bargain basement price. Once I wrap up the sale of their home, they think I am off to the next listing and the next and the next. My listing presentation changes this dynamic. As I said in the beginning of the chapter, the entire presentation gives us greater and greater credibility. The greater our credibility, the more likely they are to listen.

Beyond the credibility factor, the listing presentation tells the seller that we are all-in on the job of selling their home. By the time we get to price, they've already heard our extensive marketing plan and appreciate our investment to get the job done. Beyond money, we've told them how we plan to invest a great deal of time in marketing and showing their home ourselves. If we are going to put in this much time and money into selling their home, doesn't it make sense that we will do everything we can to maximize that investment and get as much out of their home as we possibly can? That is why we should do our entire presentation even with those who tell us they do not plan to interview anyone else. "You don't have to go to all the trouble of doing a whole presentation," they say. "We want you. The job is yours. Where do we sign? And, by the way, what do you think you can get for our home. We really think it is worth . . ."

I do my best not to take the bait. "I appreciate that," I will say, "but before we talk about price, I'd like you to hear everything I plan to do to maximize the exposure of your home to as many people as possible . . ." Even in a "come list me" situation, pricing always comes last.

Sellers are also more inclined to listen when you deliver news they may not want to hear with confidence and finesse. I graduated from Cal State, Northridge, a long time ago with a degree in communications. I don't remember most of what I learned, after all I have severe ADD and barely squeaked by with a 2.05 GPA, but one lesson has never left me. Before telling people something you know they don't want to hear, tell them something they do. This is exactly what I did with the guy who thought his home was worth an extra $50,000 because of the oak toilet seats and ceiling fans he'd installed himself. I told him how much I appreciated both items, and how I was sure that many buyers would love them. But then came what I knew he didn't want to hear: No matter how nice the toilet seats and fans might be, the price still had to fall within appraised value.

Not every seller has oak toilet seats, but many have some feature in their home they think sets it heads and shoulders above any other house in their community. It might be the landscaping or a very personalized bathroom remodel or anything else, because if you've been in this business very long, you've seen a lot of anything else. We all have. All of us probably also have tricks of the trade we've picked up along the way to convince sellers to price their home closer to market value. One of my best tools is the direct approach. When a seller is hedging, telling me they really want to try to get $2.1 or $2.2 million, I ask, "I can appreciate you wanting 2.1 or 2.2. But realistically speaking, if you were offered $2 million straight up, would you take it?" I then shut up and wait for their response. The magic answer to what we want to hear is yes, although they will likely add, "But we want more," or "I guess so."

Our response should be, "Then let's price it at $2 million. If it's worth $2 million or more" (the key words to say are *or more*), "then we will have a better chance of getting $2 million or more priced at $2 million than we will priced more than $2 million. More people will see it and therefore our odds are better at having a bidding war." I then bring them back by saying, "I cannot guarantee you we will get $2 million or more. But I guarantee you our odds are much better this way."

Hope for the Best, Prepare for the Worst

Of course, when it comes to price, we have all had clients who will not budge. No matter what we say about price, they always come back with, "Well, I'm not going to just give this place away. I won't sell for a penny less than _____." Bottom line, this is 100 percent the price we have to use. No more reasoning. No more discussions. Take it or leave it. I usually reply with something like, "I appreciate your honesty, but I would not be doing my job if I wasn't honest with you about what I think the market will bear."

Now comes decision time. Do we take an overpriced listing or walk away? This is a personal business decision you and I face all the time. I cannot lie and say that I walk away from every overpriced listing. Not all of my listings are priced right and saleable. But I can say this: I often walk away, and it hurts. I am fortunate to be in a position not to need every listing, but I'm still hungry enough to want them all. The hardest thing I do is walk away from an overpriced listing.

Whether you walk or take the overpriced listing is a personal choice with no right or wrong answer. Sometimes we feel we simply cannot say no. A listing may be in your farm, or it's a perfect ad house to capture buyers, or it is in a terrific location for heavy sign exposure. In those cases, the long-term benefits outweigh the frustration of listing a home you know will probably not sell. As long as we were honest with the sellers about our hesitations up front, then there's no ethical reason not to list something priced too high. And who knows. As sellers like to remind us, it only takes one. I like nothing more than to be proved wrong when that one unicorn comes along who pays far more than I ever thought possible for a house.

"Will You Discount Your Commission?"

The number one question I am asked is, "How do you deal with sellers who ask you to discount your commission?" Sellers ask me that just like they ask all of us. Some sellers ask because they want to feel like they got a good deal. That's basic human nature. Our goal in my listing presentation is to blow the seller away with all we plan to do and all we plan to invest to sell their home, and to do it with such confidence and professionalism, that they will see they are already getting a bargain with our 2½ percent listing side commission.* Some will still ask for a discount, but their tone of voice and the look in their eye make it clear that this is almost embarrassing for them. They ask because they feel like they are supposed to ask. Even if they don't, I bring it up. I look the seller in the eye and say:

> "Let's talk about commissions. You will see in the contract that the commission is going to be 5 percent, 2½ percent to the buyer's agent and 2½ to me."

As I say this, I skip quickly over the 5 percent and slow down when I talk about the 2½ percent to both sides. That's where I want the seller's attention because that is what I actually earn. I want them to hear the 5 percent, and listen to the 2½. Then I add:

---

* The current rate in California.

"If I represent both sides of the transaction, I am happy to do it for 4 percent. This way you will save some money, I will make a bonus, and we are all happy. And trust me, I do this often. That is one of the reasons why I will invest so much time and money to generate buyers. I want to earn that bonus by finding the right buyer that will pay your price or more."

Usually, the seller will smile and say something like, "I hope you sell it yourself, too!" which is exactly what I hope to hear.

Some of you may be wondering why I will voluntarily give up one percent of my commission. I do it to protect the 2½ percent. I also believe it's a good way to keep clients happy. Does this always work? Of course not. Remember the old saying, "Pigs get fat and hogs get slaughtered"? I am not greedy. We get paid very well to sell a house at 2½ percent per side. And when I get the full 4 percent for representing both parties, that's pretty damn awesome.

PART 2

BEYOND THE LISTING

Some Other Things I've Learned

14

BRINGING IT ALL TOGETHER

How to Break into Luxury or Any New Market

My first million-dollar sale fell in my lap purely by chance back in 1993. I happened to run into Jon, an old friend I hadn't seen since high school. After we got caught up on what had happened in our lives since graduation back in 1985, he told me I should call his twin brother, Todd. The three of us had been friends since we were kids. "He's looking at buying a million-dollar home out in Westlake Village," Jon told me. "He doesn't have an agent yet, but I know he'd love to work with you."

All I could think was, *Wow. A million-dollar home for a kid our age!* I feel lucky to own my thirteen-hundred-square-foot, old tract home with a gravel roof and no air-conditioning. In truth, I had never even been inside a million-dollar home, let alone sold one. My very next thought was, *Where is Westlake Village?*

Today, I do most of my work in Westlake Village. Back then, I didn't know a thing about it other than it had a lot of really nice, really expensive homes. The first time I went there I noticed the city had immaculate, manicured grass medians and beautifully customized wooden street signs. Also the weather was about ten degrees cooler than where I lived, and the air quality was amazing due to the breeze coming from the Pacific Ocean. I thought, *Man, I'd love to live here.*

When Jon brought up showing his brother homes in Westlake Village, I had a decision to make. I could have told my friend, "Jon, I appreciate it, but I don't work in that area. Let me connect you to an agent who does." At least once a month, maybe more, I receive referrals like this from someone who works outside my area. Either they live an hour or two away, which in Southern California can still be in the same county, or they normally sell lesser-priced homes but happened to land with a great buyer. The thought of trying to sell something outside their area or their comfort zone makes them hand off deals to agents like me.

Taking the Chance

But that's not what I did. I saw what could be a life-changing commission check right before my eyes, and I went for it. *After all*, I thought, *I may never get this opportunity again.*

"Westlake Village, oh yeah, it's amazing," I replied to Jon. He told me Todd wanted a guard-gated community. "Westlake has amazing gated communities," I said as if I knew what I was talking about. In truth, not only had I never been to Westlake Village, I didn't even know where it was.

I immediately went to work. After locating Westlake Village and learning about the gated communities they had to offer, I called Todd. Our home search was quick because I had to show

Todd and his wonderful wife, Christine, only one property. I found them a seven-thousand-square-foot mansion that was still under construction at the end of the cul-de-sac on Royal Vista Court, a prime street in guard-gated North Ranch Country Club Estates. The builder's wife acted as the listing agent, and I represented Todd and Christine. Like I said, this was the biggest sale of my life up to that point by far, and it just fell in my lap. I didn't even have to work very hard to close it. I felt very blessed, and the commission check felt like I had just won the lottery!

People ask me every day how they can break into the luxury market. This is the first step. You have to be willing to stretch yourself. When an opportunity presents itself, take it. I didn't know a thing about the area Todd and Christine were looking in, but that didn't matter. I saw this as a chance to do the deal of a lifetime, so I took it.

The only real drama with my first million-dollar deal came while we were in escrow. Early in the morning of January 17, 1994, my wife and I were asleep in our house in Chatsworth, a small city adjacent to Northridge in the San Fernando Valley. At precisely 4:30 a.m. we woke up to the ear-splitting sound of shattering windows and a crumbling fireplace. Before my brain could register what was happening, I heard what sounded like every plate and glass and dish in the kitchen crashing to the floor at the same time. My first thought: protect my wife from what might come falling down as the 6.7 earthquake nearly shook our house apart. Once I knew she was safe, my very next thought was, *Oh no. I hope Royal Vista didn't crumble.* I really, really needed that commission check.

Another Chance Meeting with Old Friends

Thankfully, the earthquake's epicenter was under Northridge, not Westlake Village. We closed on the house, and I went back to selling homes in the San Fernando Valley with a few flips of earth-quake damaged homes along the way. I can't lie, after receiving that $30,000 check from the house on Royal Vista, it was a bit of a letdown to go back to my average commission checks.

A couple years later I was walking through the Burbank airport on my way to a quick weekend in Vegas when I saw two of my oldest and best friends growing up, twin brothers David and Dana Pump. They were not hard to miss with their signature bright red hair. We hadn't seen each other in more than ten years, but we quickly caught up. I had heard through our circles of friends how successful they had become, building their basketball empire from camps and AAU travel teams. The Pumps were self-made entre-preneurs and extremely powerful in the world of basketball. I was genuinely happy for them and enjoyed the opportunity to congrat-ulate them at the airport. David then said they'd heard I was doing really well in real estate, which was quite a coincidence because they were thinking about buying their first home. Long story short, I was able to score them a steal on a foreclosure, and they were very appreciative. The best part of the deal was we were able to rekindle our friendship. Today I'm proud to say, Dana and David are two of my very best friends.

The story might have ended there, but David and Dana were and are friends through and through. They have connections with most of the players in the NBA, not to mention many other icons in the world of sports. After we closed on their home, one of their friends, a player in the NBA and a former star for my favorite col-lege, UCLA, mentioned to them that he was looking for a house. David and Dana told him, "You *have* to use our guy." They arranged a meeting, and once again, I was off to the races. Like my old friend Todd, the Player* was looking for a home somewhere

---

* Name withheld for the sake of the client's privacy.

between $1 and $2 million. He had just signed a free agent contract and was eager to buy his first home. Keep in mind that this was 1996 or 1997 when a million dollars still bought a lot of house in Southern California.

I showed the Player homes in Bel Air and other parts of the city, which were way outside my comfort zone. After looking at several but not finding what he was looking for, he said, "We ought to check out Westlake Village. Are you familiar with it?"

I said. "Heck yes. It's an incredible area. I think you'd love it."

"I've heard there are some nice gated communities there," the Player said.

Gated communities? I knew of only one, but I said, "There are some amazing gated communities there," and hoped it was true.

"Great," he said. "Let's go there."

Ready for the Spotlight?

In my first sale in Westlake Village, I interacted with only one agent, and she was from outside the area. On my second, our search for a house took longer. I met and interacted with several agents who worked only in the luxury market. Before I started looking for a home for the Player in Westlake, I assumed every agent who worked this area had to be the best of the best. After all, I'd seen their photos in the real estate section of the *Los Angeles Times* and the *Daily News* every weekend. Their sales numbers were astonishing with all the million-dollar homes they sold. I was a little intimidated and thought I might be out of my league. Two events, one at the beginning of my search and one at the end, completely changed my perspective.

I was driving my client around in my old Acura Vigor looking at homes when I remembered one in North Ranch I wanted to show him. I called the broker on my car phone and put it on speaker. An assistant answered. I told him who I was, then I said, "I have my client in my car with me, and by the way, you are on speakerphone so he and I can both hear you. I'm calling about the house on Country Valley Road, and I wanted to know how soon we could get in to see it."

"First, you will need to tell me a little about your client to make sure he qualifies," the assistant said, a very understandable question.

"Sure, no problem," I said. "I can assure you that my client is very well qualified. He is a professional athlete and ready to buy. Also, just a reminder, but you are on speakerphone and my client is here with me now."

I thought I heard a bit of a sigh before the assistant said in a very slow, almost annoyed tone of voice, "Is his wife with him as well? To show the home we will need both of them present."

"No," I said, "he is a single gentleman."

"Well," again with a tone of voice that told me the assistant felt like this call was a waste of time, he said, "Are you sure he is well qualified?" as if a single man that happens to be a professional athlete could not afford a house under two million in Westlake Village.

By this point in the conversation I was frustrated, and so was my client. Before I could open my mouth, he chimed in, "Hey man, I play in the NBA. I'm qualified to buy the house. When can we see it?!" As the Player ripped into the assistant, all I could think was, *Is this really how business is done in this price range? Man, I never would have allowed this nonsense.*

The assistant backpedaled and set up a showing. My client loved it and made an offer. But the listed price was a few hundred thousand more than he wanted to pay. I wondered if I could out-negotiate this uber successful agent and get the home for my client at the price we planned to offer.

We wrote up our offer, but rather than fax it over to the listing agent (this was the late nineties and fax machines were high tech), I insisted I be allowed to present it personally to the seller. I knew the offer was low, but I figured my best shot to get my client's offer accepted was to present it directly to the decision makers themselves. Today, where everything is done via DocuSign and email, this never happens, but I had a feeling it would work then. The listing agent, who was and is highly respected and successful, agreed to my request.

Presenting my client's offer to the seller was like walking into a listing interview for me. I was prepared. I had practiced. And I was armed with one heck of a qualified buyer. I delivered my arguments with confidence. Good or bad, the listing agent stood back and let me talk without countering. I thought for sure she would stop me or at least have me pause since her seller was visibly angry with the offer I was presenting. However, by the time I finished, I made such a compelling case that the seller accepted our offer without a counter.

On my way home from the meeting, I called my wife with my brick-sized car phone. I was on top of the world. "Honey, you are not going to believe this, but I just sold a house for $1.5 million! It's a new record for me." Both of us started screaming with joy. It was like hitting the lottery a second time. I finished the conversation by saying, "These agents over here, they're selling more than $20 million a year, and I'm selling five or six. They are all very nice, but you know what? I believe I can compete with all of them if given the chance."

"I could have told you that," she said.

"I'm serious. I think if we moved here, I could quickly make an impact and we could triple our income."

"So what are you saying?"

"I'm saying let's go for it."

"All right," she said. "I'm in!"

This conversation was not born out of arrogance. I'm not an arrogant person. We sell real estate. As I said, we are not doctors, scientists, or schoolteachers. In other words, we do not have the impact jobs to educate children or cure the sick. But I had a very high level of confidence. This was not an easy decision. The idea of moving to a new county, giving up an established real estate income that took seven years to build, and starting over was nothing to take lightly. But I had confidence in my skill set and the drive to make more money.

Becky and I soon sold our home and moved to a middle-class town called Oak Park near Westlake Village. My broker, Todd Olson, opened a tiny office for me. I didn't have a receptionist. I could not afford an assistant. Whatever needed to be done, I did it myself. None of that mattered. Not to brag, but I was young and 100 percent up for the challenge.

Our friends thought we were nuts. My friends and colleagues in the business thought we were nuts. My parents thought we were nuts. Everyone who heard what we were doing thought we were nuts. I can't blame them. We had two very young children and had just bought a house in Chatsworth. Beyond that, I was the top producer in a very successful office in the city where I grew up and certainly one of the top producers in the entire San Fernando Valley. This wasn't like working at Coca-Cola and deciding to take a job with Pepsi. Because all agents are basically self-employed, I was essentially leaving a business I had spent years building to go start something new with absolutely zero guarantee of success. I had no contacts. No friends. No repeat clients. Honestly, I barely knew how to get wherever I needed to go. But it wasn't like I was going in empty handed or had to start over completely from scratch. If you are a great real estate agent, you will be great in any market and in any city, and that's how I saw myself. I had great tools, confidence in my skill set and what I believed was an unbeatable listing presentation. I already knew how to build a geographic farm. I would put my marketing skills up against anyone. And I knew how to negotiate and close a sale. I was ready for a new challenge. With a young family and starting over, I had to work harder than my competition to make it in a new city. But I've never been afraid of hard work.

"How can I break into the luxury market?" people ask me nearly every day via social media or email. There are a few options. You can join a successful team, move to a new brokerage filled with mentors established in the luxury market, or do what I did and go all-in all alone. Either way, you have to be willing to let go of what was your bread and butter and start over in the new market. For me, this was truly an either/or decision.

I seriously believe someone selling their multimillion-dollar estate does not want to see it advertised on our websites or in newspaper ads next to $200,000 tract homes. Luxury sellers want a luxury agent who understands this market inside and out, not someone who dabbles in it. I shake my head in disbelief every time I see agents, my own competitors, to be honest, post homes or mail Just Listed or Just Solds into my marketing area promoting a small house, sometimes even a mobile home, in a completely different city. I have trouble picturing a luxury homeowner saying to themselves, "Wow, Johnny Bravo just sold a mobile home in San Bernardino. We need to interview this guy when we sell our house!" They won't. That's why you have to be all-in or all-out. I don't believe you can do both successfully.

Sometimes I ask myself how different my life might be if my first deal in Westlake Village had played out differently. Would I have moved my family and business and given up a predictable income? I seriously doubt it. But I think the only way any of us will take the bold step to move up to a larger, more competitive market is to have the confidence it takes to succeed in whatever market we enter. Confidence is not the same as pride or arrogance. Confidence is backed up by preparation, practice, and results with enough humility to know there is always room for improvement.

How Can I Stand Out in a New Market?

When I made the move to the luxury market, I went in with the goal of becoming a listing agent. As we all know, listings guarantee we make money, and the more expensive the listing, the more we make. In this new town, however, I was a complete unknown. No one selling their home had a reason to call me. Now I had to figure out how to change that.

Lake Sherwood and North Ranch and the other neighborhoods in Westlake Village did not strike me as the kinds of places where people responded well to door-to-door solicitations, which was fine with me because I never liked going door to door. I know this goes against every real estate training seminar, and every "how to increase business" YouTube video, but I personally hate it. Disturbing people during lunch or dinner to hand out trick-or-treat bags or a notepad was not my thing. Plus, I never looked at door-to-door solicitation as professional. When the day comes that doctors and lawyers start going door to door to drum up business, that's when I will do the same. Nor did I believe people who lived in multimillion-dollar homes would pay much attention to a bulk-mailed postcard from some new guy proclaiming he was now available to sell their homes especially when I was competing with experienced and well-established professionals. A luxury market called for a more upscale, out of the box approach, and I had an idea.

I sat down and wrote out a long letter of introduction that I planned to send out to all thousand homes in my chosen new farm,

North Ranch.* I spent countless hours working on it to get it just right. To make the first impression I hoped to make, this letter had to be both personal and informative, detailed yet readable. This had to be a letter that recipients would read thoroughly from top to bottom. By the time they reached the end, I wanted eyes opened and eyebrows raised and the reader thinking, *This is incredible. I never thought about real estate agents like this before.*

My broker at the time warned me that my letter was too long. "No one is going to read the whole thing," he said, and he was probably right if this had been a mass mailer. But I did not plan to send out a bulk mail letter. Instead, I went out and bought the best stationary I could find, including special linen envelopes. I then printed out a thousand copies of the same letter, one at a time, each personally addressed to the homeowner. I then hand signed each one. Rather than slap a sticker on the envelopes, I hired a sixteen-year-old kid with perfectly scripted handwriting skills to handwrite and address each and every envelope. I could have saved money with bulk mail stamps, but I bought first class instead. Every single letter then looked like a personal letter of introduction sent only to the addressee and no one else. I was sure everyone who received it would at least open it, if not read the whole thing. I also printed the words, "Recent Comparables Enclosed," along the bottom of every envelope. The sheet of comps was easy to read and easy to follow so that any layperson could understand them. I printed each comp sheet individually, so they would not look copied.

I probably spent at least a month writing and rewriting that letter until I had it exactly the way I wanted it. I wish I still had a copy of it today. Basically, the letter was like a mini listing

---

* In my next book I will go much deeper into farming, including how to choose the right farm.

presentation. I also made it clear that I had a long track record of success in a different market and that my goal was to be their new agent of choice. "Just interview me and see that I bring a new and more aggressive approach to real estate," I wrote.

Not long after the letter went out, I received my first invitation to come out and interview for a listing. Before I could begin my listing presentation, the homeowner asked, "How did you know we were getting ready to put our home on the market?" My goal had been to make everyone who received this letter believe I had written it just for them, and this seller's response told me I had hit my mark. I won that listing along with two more interviews that came as a direct result of my introductory letter. I could not have been happier. For those of you who also believe successful geographical farming is a guaranteed way to make money in this business, try the personal letter. I really hope it works as well for you as it did for me.

Game On

Since I was brand new in Westlake, I did a broker's open house with my very first listing. I wanted to expose my listing to all the other agents in the area and make some new real estate friends. You never get a second chance to make a first impression, so I upped my game. I hired a coffee truck and served delicious finger sandwiches from Brent's Deli. When people came to the door, I greeted them dressed in my best suit with a big smile on my face. Most were very nice, but I could feel questioning looks from a handful. No one knew my name. No one knew the Todd C. Olson brokerage. No one knew my track record. To them I was a completely unknown entity. But no one said anything. Everyone was too polite for that . . . with one exception.

About halfway through the open house a broker walked up to me, gave me the once-over, and said with a very dismissive tone, "How did *you* get this listing? Are you related to them or something?"

I kept the smile on my face, but inside a flame was lit and I became angry. "No, we're not related," I said. "I got the listing the same way we all do. I interviewed for it, and they went with me."

"Oh," she said with a snort. She flipped her hair and walked away. She had to be wondering what on earth convinced them to interview me in the first place, but she didn't ask.

As I watched her leave, all I could think was, Game on, lady. You just messed with the wrong cowboy!

After that, I had one goal: dominate this market. The old adage says to know the competition, and I set out to learn more about the other agents in this area than they knew about themselves. I studied every mailer they sent out, every advertisement they placed in every publication, every description they wrote for their listings, and I elevated to the next level. Everyone else sent out Just Listed postcards. That's when I started doing full-color brochures in custom envelopes. Every other agent sent out promotional mailers once a month; I did them once a week with thicker cardstock and higher-quality printing. My credit cards were maxed out, and I could not afford to pay even one assistant, but that didn't matter. I was out to establish myself in this market as *the* guy you needed if you were serious about selling your home. I did not have a fancy office. I did not have any kind of staff for the first several years. I just had a great listing presentation and confidence.

My presence in that market took off very quickly and grew steadily over the years. I worked very, very hard, using everything I wrote about in this book, and I still do today. I do top-quality photographs and videos. I do Just Listed brochures. I do strategic, well-placed, full-page ads. I do Just Sold mailers. I do all that I promise in my listing presentation, which turns into houses selling and people calling asking if I could do for them what I had done for their neighbor. The system works because it's not a system. For me, it is putting my clients first, looking at the sale of their home through their eyes, and producing results. If we will do that, we will be successful.

Co-listings as a Way In

My introduction to the luxury market came as a buyer's agent, but that's not the only way you can enter. If you have a lead on a luxury listing and know you will have to go up against some of the heavy hitters to win it, contacting a top agent in that market to co-list with you is a great way to get your foot in the door. For me, a co-list is a potential listing I would not have had any other way. Half of something is better than a whole of nothing.

Surprisingly, most agents who call me from outside my marketing area don't ask about co-listing. They call to refer a client to me. I gladly accept, but I always see that as a missed opportunity for them. I never pass up those opportunities. I've called top local agents about co-listing opportunities I've had in Florida, Colorado, Montana, even Whistler, Canada, or anywhere else a door opens up.

About ten years ago I was on the receiving end of one of these terrific co-list opportunities. I got a call from a broker smart enough not to refer out a listing just because he did not normally work in an area. This was literally the first time not only that I was asked to co-list but also the first time I interviewed side by side with another broker.

I answered the phone and the voice on the other end said, "Hey, is this Jordan Cohen?"

"Yep."

"This is Josh Altman." I recognized the name from the reality show *Million Dollar Listing*, but I honestly had never seen the show. I lived real estate every day. The last thing I wanted to do when I got home was watch people selling real estate on television. That said, Josh was already well known and respected by every Los Angeles real estate agent by his name and reputation.

"Okay," I said.

"How you doing, man?" he said with a direct tone. "I don't know you and I don't really know who you are, but people tell me you're kind of a big deal in the Valley around Hidden Hills."

This sounded a little like a backhanded compliment. I answered with, "Well, Josh, I appreciate the call, but is there something you want from me?"

"Listen," he said, "I have a possible co-list opportunity for a big house in Hidden Hills. I don't know if you do that sort of thing, but like I said, I heard you were kind of a big deal in that area, so I thought I'd ask."

All the houses in Hidden Hills are big houses. Lots of celebrities call it home, and I'd sold several over the years. That was why Josh was calling. He works out of Beverly Hills, which is quite the drive from Hidden Hills. He needed a local agent like me to handle showings and the day-to-day needs of the sellers. Josh's call had quickly become a money call, and all was great.

"You know, Josh, I really appreciate you calling me. Yeah man, I'd love to do this with you," I said. Opportunity was knocking, a sound I never turn down.

"Okay, great. So I have a listing interview appointment with the seller Friday at noon. We'll both go, but I'll take the lead. That work for you?"

"Yeah. Sounds good. I'll see you then."

A couple days later, Josh and I arrived at the potential listing at the same time. I pulled up in whatever car I happened to own at the time. I don't even remember what it was. Josh arrived in a shiny Rolls-Royce. *Man*, I thought, *this dude rolls big.* He opened his car door and stepped out. He looked every bit like a television star with his spiked-up hair and suntan. He was rocking a skin-tight, form-fitted, purple suit, shiny new shoes that looked like he just took them out of the box in the car, black belt with a gold Gucci buckle, and the strong scent of freshly applied expensive cologne. Me? I wore my regular work attire consisting of a button-down shirt and jeans. But I did throw on a tweed sports coat since I knew it was an expensive house.

I walked over to Josh, put out my hand and said, "Hey, Josh, Jordan, nice to meet you man."

"Yeah, nice to meet you, too."

The two of us started walking to the house. About halfway up the drive I said, "Josh, I've got to tell you something. Even though I've been doing this for years, this is the first time I have ever gone on a co-listing interview appointment with another agent."

Josh swung around, gave me a little smile, shot me a finger gun, and said, "And you're doing it with a legend!"

Oh my God, I thought, *am I doing this interview with another real estate agent or am I doing it with Tom Cruise?* I didn't know whether to laugh out loud or get in my car and leave. Instead I froze for a moment in disbelief. After the comedic shock wore off, I said something like, "Okay," and followed him up to the house. To be honest, I was speechless in a funny way.

After the seller gave us a tour of their home, we started the listing interview. Josh went first. He immediately earned my respect. He was polished and highly skilled, threw out some great stuff and graciously handed over the baton to me. I took it from there since I knew I would be the day-to-day primary point of contact for the sellers. I gave it my all. I pulled out every tool in my toolbox and delivered the same presentation that had won me more than a thousand listings through the years. Not only did I know the sellers were engaged, I could tell by the look on Josh's face that he not only saw and heard new stuff, but he was completely blown away and shocked at my presentation.

We won the listing, and in the process, I won Josh's respect, just as he won mine. The two of us have, along with his equally skilled brother, Matt, become the best of real estate friends and have worked together on many deals. Josh and Matt are two of the best agents I've ever met. They earn and deserve all their success. From time to time I retell the story of how Josh and I first met, and every time he nearly wets himself laughing.

That's the beauty of co-listing opportunities. Not only can it open the door for a new market, but it can, as it did for me, build treasured relationships. And I think that's the greatest part of being in the business, no matter what market you are in. Yes, the pay can be great, but the people we meet are even better. In my thirty-plus years, I've met some special ones, as you will read about in the next chapter.

One Final Word About Luxury Markets

Reading all of these stories, you may think that the only way to prove yourself as a real estate agent is to keep climbing the ladder until you reach the ultraluxury market, as if luxury is the big leagues and everything else is the minors. Nothing could be further from the truth. Some of the very best agents and brokers I know, some of the icons in the business, have never had the desire to leave the markets they dominate, and I am glad they don't. I would hate to go up against them day in and day out. People like Stephanie Vitacco, who was the number one Keller Williams agent in the world, are sharp, polished, and can succeed anywhere. Stephanie and I started out in the San Fernando Valley around the same time. I moved to Westlake Village, but she stayed in the Valley and absolutely kills it. Again, that's one of the things I love about real estate. You can choose to live and work wherever works best for you and your family. A great agent is a great agent, whether they sell homes in Beverly Hills, California, or Bangor, Maine, or anywhere in between.

15

THE PEOPLE BUSINESS

I started off this book by saying that real estate is the only profession I know that gives you the opportunity for unlimited income while letting you choose your own hours. It's a great career choice because you don't have to start off at the bottom and slowly work your way up. You can take your career as far and as fast as you want. My life is proof of that. That's why I love what I do. But that's not the best part of this job. Yes, you can make a lot of money if that is your goal. And you can make a name for yourself within your market. Who would have believed thirty years ago that you could become a television star by selling houses? That's just nuts, but I have friends who have done it, and I'm thrilled for them. Television is not really my thing, but even if I had my own show, that still would not be the best part of what I do.

The best part of selling residential real estate, the one thing that has enriched my life and my family's life beyond our wildest imagination, are the relationships and friendships I've discovered along the way. You never know what may grow out of the time you spend with people, working with them on one of the most personal decisions they will make. That's why I chose residential over commercial real estate. Commercial is all about analytics. Find the space, crunch the numbers, sign the papers, cash the check, move on to the next deal. With residential, you become a part of a family's life. Finding the right home is not about checking off boxes with the right number of bedrooms and bathrooms in the right neighborhood at the right price. Buying and selling a home is an emotional decision. Buyers just know when a house feels right, like this could be the place where their family's next set of memories will grow. Sellers travel down the opposite road. Turning loose of the place where their children were born, walking away from that front yard where their oldest child took her first steps, saying goodbye to that space behind the kitchen door where parents have marked their children's height year after year—none of that comes easily. Even when a family has outgrown a home or a couple finds it is time to downsize, you cannot take the emotional element out of the process.

And when you walk down that emotional road with buyers and sellers, you can form a bond. Obviously not every time. Many deals may be nothing more than a sale where you get along great through the process but struggle to remember to keep in touch afterward so that they will remember you the next time they decide to buy or sell. But there are those clients with whom you do more than list their house or take them to one showing after another. You connect. Walls come down as you prove through the deal that you really do have their best interests at heart. More than that, for whatever reason, a friendship forms. To me, those are the deals that have given me the amazing life I've had the pleasure to have lived. I often find myself sitting back wondering how I got here, which is why I never take any of these friendships for granted. I treasure them all. Because of the market in which I work, many of these friends have names you will recognize. A few have even granted me permission to share a small part of our story together. But I know that if I had never transitioned into the luxury market and had spent all of the past thirty-plus years in the San Fernando Valley, I would still have stories to tell with names no one but me would recognize. I know this because, as one of my good friends once told me, "Jordan, you aren't in the house selling business. You are in the people business." That friend was NFL Hall of Famer Marcus Allen, one of the greatest guys I've ever had the pleasure to have met and worked for. But that first meeting almost didn't happen, not because of him, but because of me.

Marcus Allen

A friend of mine who was very prominent in the NFL, a guy named Mike, called one day about one of his clients. Mike and I did a couple deals together and had known one another for quite a while. Any time he called me with a referral made for a great day. And this was a really great day. Mike told me he'd like for me to broker a transaction on a house in Montecito near Santa Barbara for Marcus Allen. Marcus and the buyer, another football legend, Troy Aikman, were good friends. This was basically a handshake deal where the house never actually went on the market. "I told Marcus you were the perfect guy to walk them through the entire process through closing," Mike said.

When I heard the name Marcus Allen, my mind went, *Holy shit!* I'd worked with many athletes and celebrities by this point in my career. I counted some as friends. But man, this name, Marcus Allen, was special. I grew up a rabid football fan in the seventies and eighties in Southern California, and Marcus Allen *was* football! He won the Heisman Trophy at USC in 1981 for rushing for an unbelievable twenty-three hundred yards. Then, when the Raiders moved to LA from Oakland before the 1982 season, they drafted Marcus in the first round. All he did in his eleven years with the Raiders was win the Rookie of the Year award *and* a Most Valuable Player award *and* a Super Bowl in which he was named the Super Bowl MVP! Of course he was a first ballot Hall of Famer. The hall was made specifically for players like Marcus Allen. Two years after he left the Raiders, the team packed up and moved back to Oakland. While he was here, he owned this town. No one was bigger. Even Magic Johnson, the Lakers' biggest star, stood on the sidelines of Raider games to watch Marcus play. This guy was a legend both on the field and off. And now Mike had referred him to me. *Holy shit!*

I pulled myself together and told Mike, "Of course, I'll broker the deal." Mike thanked me and set up a meeting.

When the day came to meet Marcus personally, I left my office, put the top down on my car, and headed up the 101 for the hour-long drive to Montecito. I wish the drive had been shorter because the longer I was in the car, the more time I had to think about what was about to happen. *I'm going to meet Marcus Allen. No big deal. I've represented many celebrities*, I told myself. And told myself. And told myself. About halfway up the coast it hit me: *Marcus Allen isn't just a celebrity. He is one of my heroes! Oh shit, I am about to meet one of my greatest sports heroes. How can I do that?!*

I felt like I had just stepped into a scene from *The Sopranos*. My heart started racing. I couldn't catch my breath. I'd never had a panic attack before, but that had to be what I was feeling: sheer panic. Quickly I pulled my car over to the shoulder of the freeway, put it into park, and sat there for at least thirty minutes trying to regain some kind of control of myself. I ended up having to call Marcus to tell him I was going to be a little late. I was too embarrassed to tell him what had actually happened, so I blamed the one thing you can always blame for being late in Southern California: traffic.

Nearly an hour after our scheduled meeting time, I pulled into Marcus's driveway. He met me outside. Even though he had retired from football a few years earlier, the guy looked like he could step right back onto the field and still rush for two thousand yards. He stepped over and shook my hand. "Hey, Jordan. Marcus. Nice to meet you," he said. It was a quick meeting. We signed the contracts, opened escrow, and closed the deal without a hitch. Working with him exceeded all my expectations and we became fast friends.

Since the sale of his house went so smoothly, Marcus asked me to help him search for a place in Los Angeles to rent until he decided where he wanted to buy. I found a penthouse apartment with amazing 360-degree views on the top floor of a building in the middle of Hollywood Hills. Places like this never came up for rent, but this one had so I knew we needed to get over to see it quickly. We walked in, and I have to say, there is nothing like walking into a room with Marcus Allen. When he played football, he didn't run over people. He glided down the field. His playing days may be over, but he carries himself in the same way. He just has a presence about him, like the embodiment of Southern California cool.

We walked into the apartment. Marcus took a look around, then looked over toward me. "Jordan, I have to tell you man, this place is perfect." He then looked over at the listing agent doing the showing. "I'll take it," Marcus said.

Apparently the listing agent had never watched football. "Oh no, no, no, that's not how this works," he said. "You need to go back with your agent to his office and have him write up a formal proposal and provide us a copy of your financial qualifications and credit. Your agent will then submit it. In due time the owner will review all the proposals and make his determination."

Marcus looked at me, a little surprised, but he remained calm, the very picture of cool. "No, I don't think you understand what I'm saying," Marcus replied. "I have plenty of money and perfect credit. If the owner wants, I'll pay the full year of rent right up front. Whatever he's asking for it, I'll take it."

The other agent wasn't having any of it. He straightened up to his full five-foot, five-inches, puffed out his flabby chest and said with a voice dripping with arrogance and attitude, "No, Mr. Allen, you are the one who does not understand. We have a procedure to follow here. Other parties are interested in this apartment. Are you familiar with the actress Laura Dern? She was just here, and she had some interest in the apartment as well. That is why you must submit a proposal through your agent and the *owner* will determine to whom he chooses to rent this property."

I have now known Marcus for a very long time. I consider him a very dear friend. He embodies class and sophistication. I can count on one finger the number of times I have seen him angry. And that's what makes the rest of the story so funny to me.

After the listing agent finished his little speech, Marcus looked around, incredulous. He then looked the agent in the eye and said a few choice words that made it very clear his patience had worn out. Marcus then said, "Who is the owner? What's his name?"

The other agent, now nervous and embarrassed, sort of mumbled a name, shocked that he'd just been put in his place by a living legend.

"I know him. Get him on the phone. Let's wrap this up now," Marcus said.

The agent dialed the number, said hello, then handed the phone to Marcus. I stood back and took it all in. Marcus and the owner talked for a short time, smiling, laughing, like two old friends.

After a few moments, Marcus handed the phone back to the agent. "Here you go," he said.

The next conversation was quite entertaining. I can imagine what the apartment owner was saying by the response of the agent. "Okay. Okay. Okay. Yes. Thank you." He then hung up the phone and said, "Mr. Allen, the place is yours." If the agent had known a little more about the owner of the property, he could have saved himself a phone call. The owner was an icon in Hollywood . . . and a USC alum. Trust me when I say that Marcus Allen is arguably the most beloved USC Trojan of all time. My guess is the owner was more excited to have Marcus as a tenant than Marcus was to rent the place.

After that Marcus and I became really close friends. Word got out in the community where my family and I lived that I had some high-profile clients. Every time the grade school or middle school or high school or any other organization in town had a fundraiser, someone called me asking for silent auction items. They still do to this day. One of the first times this happened, I was very open to the idea. After all, I want to do what I can to make our community better. So I called Marcus and asked if he would sign a few footballs for me. "Jordan, for you, anything," he replied. Great. I stopped by a sporting goods store, bought eight footballs, then drove over to his place with a Sharpie in hand. When he saw eight footballs, he asked, "Are all these for you?"

"No," I said, "they're for silent auctions and some friends."

Marcus sort of nodded and said, "Jordan, man, I'm going to give you a little advice because we're friends. Now I will sign these balls for you. You're my friend and I am happy to do it. But you're a great guy and you're great at what you do. Your business is going to grow, and you'll meet a lot more athletes. But here's the thing, don't ask athletes or any of your other celebrity clients for autographs or anything like that. As soon as you do, you cross the line from friend to fan. For me and you, it's different. Now, you and me, we're friends no matter what. But let me tell you, you never want to be that guy that's always asking for favors."

I had never even thought about that. I was both embarrassed and grateful. I took his words to heart. Today, I follow his advice no matter who I am representing.

As Marcus signed the footballs, he looked up at me and said, "This silent auction, it's a fundraiser, right?"

"For my son's high school football team."

"If you really want these footballs to bring in some big numbers, let me call my good friend, Eric Dickerson, and I'll get him to sign them, too." My jaw dropped. Eric Dickerson just happens to be one of the greatest running backs in NFL history as a star for both the Rams and the Indianapolis Colts. Two Hall of Fame signatures on one ball were epic, especially here in Los Angeles. Needless to say, those footballs turned out to be the most popular items in the silent auction. The next year Marcus did me one better. He volunteered to be the keynote speaker at the same high school football fundraiser. The event sold out immediately. Once again, my friend did me a solid. It's hard to find a better friend or a better person than Marcus Allen.

Marcus also told me something about myself that I never realized before he said it. He told me, "Jordan, the way you do your job, you aren't in the real estate business. You are in the people business." He was right, not just about me but about all of us. We really are in the people business.

Sylvester Stallone

I had never had a panic attack until the day I met Marcus Allen. That was just the warm-up for what came next.

I was exiting the 101 freeway off Van Nuys Boulevard when my phone rang. I recognized the number as belonging to a business manager I had worked with on deals for his clients. As soon as I answered, his secretary said, "Jordan, I have Sylvester Stallone for you. I'm going to connect you now." The business manager and I had spoken a couple days earlier, so I was expecting the call. But expecting it and receiving it were two very different experiences.

And then I heard the voice. "Hey, Jordan. How ya doing?" I had to pull over and stop my car. It was like an out-of-body experience. For me, there was no one bigger in the entire world. No bigger sports star. No bigger television star. No bigger movie star. Sylvester Stallone had been my favorite actor since I went to see *Rocky* with my parents, and the *Rocky* series is my favorite of all time. To this day I watch them all twice a year. And now the Italian Stallion himself was on the phone with me. *Me! How did this happen?*

We talked for several minutes. He explained how he wanted to find a summer beach rental for himself and his family. I had to force myself not to lose it listening to him. I mean, that voice is so distinctive, so powerful. He went on to tell me about his family and what they were looking for. The more we talked the more it became like a normal conversation with a guy who loved his family and wanted to spend quality time with them in a special place. I told him I had a couple places where I could look, and I'd line up some properties to show him. He thanked me and said he looked forward to meeting in person. "Me too," I said. When I hung up the phone, I sat there in my car for several minutes trying to wrap my brain around the idea that I was going to meet my true childhood hero.

I went to work looking for properties. I found one I thought might work, and we arranged a time for me to show it to him and his wonderful wife, Jennifer. When the day came, I woke up, looked over at my wife, and literally felt sick. I have never been that nervous in my life, and I don't know if I ever will again. After I showered and got dressed, I felt even worse. *Maybe I just need some coffee*, I told myself. I decided to make a quick pit stop at Starbucks on my way over to the property. But I didn't make it. As I drove up Kanan Road, my head started spinning and my stomach started doing flips. I pulled over quickly, hung my head out my door, and I really hate to admit it in this book, but I started throwing up. I wasn't sick. It was nerves. You have to keep in mind: I've met many famous people. I've met actors and athletes and rock stars and every other kind of celebrity, but I never reacted like this before or since. But there was something about meeting a man that in my mind was bigger than life that completely overwhelmed me. I ended up calling Jennifer and telling her a bullshit story that I had food poisoning and would not be able to make the showing. The listing agent covered for me by doing a courtesy showing. With my tail between my legs, I turned my car around and went home, nauseated and embarrassed.

The old saying goes we never get a second chance to make a first impression, but I almost never even got a first chance. As you can probably tell by Sly's writing the foreword for this book, we did meet and became friends. It wasn't until he offered to write the foreword that I told him the story of me getting sick on my way over to meet him. He laughed so hard that he pulled out a phone and did a video of the two of us together. It wasn't the first video he did for me, which is a story in itself.

I am writing this chapter on a day that feels like much more than a coincidence. Tomorrow morning my wife and I will fly to New York for our daughter's graduation from the New York University Tisch School of the Arts, one of the top film schools in the world. A couple of years back, while showing Sly some properties, I mentioned something about a special effects class my daughter Cassidy was taking at the time. She had sent me some photos of the movie makeup she'd created, and I thought it was phenomenal. Of course, I am supposed to think that since I'm her dad, but I still thought it was really, really good. I asked Sly to take a look and tell me what he thought. He took my phone and didn't just look at the photos. He studied them. When he handed me back my phone, he said with all sincerity, "Jordan, she's got it. Her work in these pictures is better than some of the special effects makeup created by artists working in the industry right now. Yeah, she's just amazing. Jordan, I think your daughter has a great future ahead of her."

Now, Sly could have just been being polite. After all, what was he supposed to say in that situation? But he didn't say this like he was blowing smoke. In the moment he felt quite sincere. Later that night my phone buzzed. I had a video message from Sly that he shot in his home office. But the message wasn't for me. It was for Cassidy. In the video he told her he was a good friend of her dad and that I had shown him her work. He then told her basically what he had told me. As he did, he turned the camera around and showed her part of his collection of masks and other effects and props from his movie career. He concluded his video with some practical advice on what steps to take next to get established in the business. "Keep it up," he said, "follow your dreams. You have a bright future ahead of you."

After watching the video, I sat back in my chair in utter shock and awe. Here was not only my favorite actor of all time speaking directly to my daughter to encourage and motivate her, but he is also one of the most iconic actors of our time. I had no words except to say thanks. I forwarded the video on to Cassidy. To this day she rewatches it on a regular basis. And this week, a few days after I write these words, she will graduate from film school. The only thing that will make this story better is if she gets to work with Sly on a film someday. As I think about all of this, I can only say, *How did I get here?* Again, the answer is very basic. We are in the people business. Real estate is all about relationships, and those relationships are bigger than any deals we might make.

John Ryan

One of my favorite parts of what we do are the relationships we build with one another as fellow real estate agents. We may compete against one another for listings, but we are anything but adversaries. I've built some incredible friendships with others in the business both around the Los Angeles area and around the world. These friendships have inspired and changed me, none more so than a guy I only met because he did something none of us ever do: he answered his phone while on vacation in Hawaii to a call from a number he did not recognize. I'm glad he did, because John Ryan is one of the most inspiring people I know, and a great friend.

I had no idea who John was late one Saturday afternoon when I first called him. In fact, I wasn't even looking for houses in his primary area. That day started out a thousand miles away in Montana. I'd flown up there with wealthy clients on their private jet in search of a winter home. I thought I'd found them the perfect place, but we arrived to see it on a gray, dreary day, which only made the brown, snowless hills surrounding the house that much less inviting. The house itself was nice enough, but I could tell by the looks in my clients' eyes that this wasn't *the* house. On the flight back to Los Angeles, they turned to me and asked, "So Jordan, where else should we look?"

The question was harder than it appears. I'd sold this couple a home in the Rocky Mountains a few years earlier, but the elevation wasn't conducive. The foothills of Montana seemed to fit the bill, but now that we'd crossed that off the list I had to scramble to come up with someplace new. Then it hit me: my brother has been a cameraman for nearly thirty-five years. He has worked on hundreds of movies and television shows and has worked all over the world. A couple years earlier he'd shot a movie up in Whistler, British Columbia, and came back blown away. He told me how beautiful the area was with its mountain views, while the elevation was under three thousand feet. That made it the best of both worlds. "What about Canada?" I asked. I then told them what my brother had said about Whistler. "It's not that far up there, and the views are supposed to be incredible," I said.

My clients liked the idea. They started scrolling through homes in Whistler on their laptops and landed on two that looked promising. "You think we could fly up and see these two tomorrow?" they asked.

I glanced at my watch. It was already four in the afternoon. By the time we landed in Los Angeles it would be too late to call the listing agent, much less line anything up for the next day. I wasn't sure how I could pull that off. My clients must have seen the concern on my face because they told me they had a phone in the back of the plane I could use right then. I still wasn't too hopeful, but it was worth a shot. I called the listing agent of the first house. The agent answered quickly. "Hello, this is John Ryan."

"Hello, John," I said, "you don't know me. My name is Jordan Cohen and I'm a real estate broker out of Los Angeles. I know this may sound a little crazy, but I'm calling you from the back of an airplane owned by one of my biggest clients, and we'd like to come up and see a couple of your properties tomorrow if that is at all possible."

"Sure, no problem, buddy. I'm in Hawaii right now, but let me give you my assistant's number and she will set everything up for you," he said in the coolest, most nonchalant way as though he received calls from the back of private jets every day. He didn't ask who my client was or what they did, which I would have done.

Instead, he accommodated this strange request like he had known me all his life.

As it turned out, a heavy winter storm in Whistler kept us from flying up the next day. Instead we set everything up for the following weekend, which worked out even better since it allowed John to be there in person. He helped arrange for a helicopter to meet my clients and me at the Vancouver airport to fly us up to Whistler. At this point, the only thing I knew about John Ryan was that he was one of the top real estate agents in Canada. Like me, he specialized in luxury properties. From talking to him on the phone I also knew he was a hell of a nice guy.

The following Sunday we made the trip up north. Before our helicopter landed in Whistler, I knew this was the place. I've been in many beautiful places in the world, but I have to say I have never seen anything more beautiful in my life than the view out the helicopter window from Vancouver to Whistler. It was the most breathtaking scenery imaginable. We all felt it.

As we exited the helicopter in Whistler, a man rolled up in a wheelchair, a big smile on his face. One look told me this man was a free spirit. He rolled over to me, put out his hand, and said, "Hi. I'm John Ryan."

It didn't take me long to figure out why John Ryan is Whistler's number one real estate agent. But he's more than that. The guy is a legend north of the border. As I got to know him, I learned a car wreck in 1994 left him paralyzed from the waist down, but it barely slowed him down. In 1999 he pedaled his handcycle bike from St. John's, Newfoundland, all the way across Canada to Whistler. That's only fifty-four hundred miles! He did it to raise money for spinal cord injury research. The day we met I was impressed at how he rolled up steep driveways in the Canadian cold, always with a smile, always with a tremendous attitude.

Then I learned about what he called his Regeneration Tour. I've never met anyone like him.

John and I became fast friends. I have to be honest. I am in awe of him. I've watched him in action. I see how he is with people. I can tell you stories about how he goes above and beyond with every client. To this day, when I've had a shitty day and I'm feeling sorry for myself, I think about John spending 130 days traveling fifty-four hundred miles on a hand bike, and I kick myself in the ass. I am grateful every day to call John and his sensational team my friends.

I could write several more books filled with stories of the amazing people who have touched my life as a direct result of my job. I am sure we can all do the same. Many are household names, people like Aaron Donald, Anthony Davis, and Bret Michaels. Others, like John Ryan, you have never heard of, but their impact is just as strong. Again, this is my favorite part of my career in real estate. Yes, it's given my family and me incredible opportunities and an incredible life. When I started out with the Todd C. Olson brokerage straight out of college thirty-plus years ago, I never could have dreamed what the future had in store for me. But the best part, the part I would not trade for all the money in the world, is the friendships I've made and the relationships that have formed over something as simple as selling a house. That's why we do what we do. This is the people business, and we are the ones who reap the greatest benefit.

ACKNOWLEDGMENTS

I realize this could quite possibly be the longest acknowledgments chapter in the history of books. But I am just a real estate agent, and this is my golden opportunity to publicly thank the people who have truly helped me throughout my career. I am sure there are a lot of you reading this who are saying, "I can't believe this guy is thanking everyone from his mold inspector to his plumber. I'm going to close the book now." Or "Good for him for thanking so many people. I would do the same thing." In any event, this is the part of the book I am most excited about writing.

The first person I am excited to thank is the legendary Mark Tabb. Mark is an award-winning author whom I was lucky enough to land as my collaborator on this book. We spent hundreds of hours both in person in his hometown of Indianapolis and also on Zoom. The principles, strategies, and stories in the book are all mine, but it all came together so eloquently because of Mark. Not only was Mark a pleasure to work with every day, but more importantly I feel like I made a friend for life. I hope we can continue this journey with a series of books!

The next person I would love to thank is Elan Ruspoli. There is no chance this book would ever have been written without Elan.

Elan is a mega Hollywood agent, client, and friend. I was fortunate to sell Elan and his beautiful wife, Jacqueline, a house in Westlake Village, while at the same time selling their previous home in the Hollywood Hills. Elan said, "You are so good at this, you should write a book on it." I said, "I have actually thought about it for many years." He said, "I will introduce you to one of our literary agents. My guess is he would love to represent you." Thank you, Elan! You are an amazing person and friend, and I will be forever grateful.

Another person that I owe everything to is my agent, Anthony Mattero, and CAA. First of all, it's awkward to even say "my agent" because I'm a real estate agent, nothing more, nothing less, but I must admit, it's bad ass at the same time! People like me do not have an "agent," let alone the biggest on the planet with CAA, but without Anthony and CAA, I would never have received the book deal with HarperCollins Leadership. Anthony is another person I will now consider a lifelong friend. Thank you, Anthony, for taking a chance on me, and thank you for your incredible negotiating skills, connections, and patience. It's been an honor to work with you through the process.

Of course, none of this would have happened without the incredible leadership team at HarperCollins Leadership. Most important, Tim Burgard. I am so incredibly grateful, Tim. Thank *you* for everything! Talk about taking a chance. Tim read my twenty-page treatment, had a Zoom call with me, and based on that alone, signed a relatively unknown real estate agent to write a playbook on "how to sell real estate." I'm not a reality TV star with a built-in following. I'm not a trainer or a "coach." I'm simply a real estate agent busting my ass every day to sell as many homes as possible, and HarperCollins Leadership made the investment in me and my story. I sure hope my book sells well so I do not let Tim and his amazing team down. Thank you.

I also want to thank Sicily Axton at HarperCollins Leadership. Sicily is the expert promoter and spearheaded the launch and marketing for my book. Thank you, Sicily.

Most important, I *have* to thank all my clients. Over thirty-two years I've had the honor to work for some of the greatest people imaginable. I don't want to sound like a "salesperson" and give corny thank-yous, but it's so true. To all the people who have trusted me with the sale of not only their most important financial asset but their family home, thank you. I obviously would not be in business without you. I wish I could list everyone here, but I cannot. But there are a few clients that I would love to thank.

My very first "heartfelt" thank you begins with Kobe and Vanessa Bryant. What was my big break? That is the easiest question and answer I have. My biggest break came when I was referred to Kobe and Vanessa. I am honored to say for more than twenty years I have not only been fortunate enough to call them remarkable clients but, more important, friends. Thank you, V! Thank you for your loyalty, trust, and friendship. You and Kobe changed my life in more ways than one, and I will be forever grateful.

Sylvester and Jennifer Stallone—this is as big as it gets for me! Not only are Sly and Jennifer incredibly loyal, but to say I am friends with my hero is an understatement. I get it: all of us wish we could befriend our favorite actor, and I'm blessed to have done it. When Sly agreed to write my foreword, I knew I hit the lottery. His heart-warming foreword is one of the nicest things anyone has ever done for me! Thank you Sly, thank you Jennifer . . . for everything.

I cannot write a book without thanking two incredible people who also changed my life: Thomas and Alba Tull. Through countless transactions, we developed a friendship that supersedes business. I hope you know how important you are to me. Thanks for truly elevating my business and life!

I would also like to thank one of my best friends, who also happens to be one of my best clients, Ron Sentchuk. Every real estate agent dreams of landing at least one mega developer, and Ron is my guy. Ron and I grew up in the Valley together and both went to Granada Hills High School. I ran into Ron many years after high school and learned he became a developer. I have sold dozens of luxury estates for Ron and am grateful for each one. Another lifelong friend!

I want to also thank Pete and Bridgette Sampras. The Samprases have been epic clients of mine for many years. Their loyalty to me is so much appreciated, whether it's in Beverly Hills or Thousand Oaks. The Samprases have entrusted their real estate with me. Their generosity is also unmatched. I am so grateful to not only call them amazing clients but friends.

I want to also thank my dear friends Anthony and Marlen Davis. What started out as business has evolved into friendship. Calling one of the NBA's best a friend is pretty awesome, but they are much more. Thanks guys, for everything.

As I mentioned, I wish I could thank the approximately two thousand clients I have worked for in my thirty-two years in the business, but the publisher won't let me. Here are a few, however. I would like to thank Dan Selleck. Dan, like so many others, interviewed me to sell his estate in Lake Sherwood. He hired me and we have had a special run together since. I sold his Sherwood Estate for a record-breaking price per square foot at the time. And we recently sold his North Ranch Estate, which shattered more records. Dan is a local legend. Developing shopping centers and real estate and landing him as a client was a big deal in my local market. Thanks for the biz, Dan, and even better, thanks for the friendship.

I have to thank the greatest of all time, LA Rams star and three-time defensive player of the year Aaron Donald and his amazing wife, Erica. I'm a lifelong Rams fan and season ticket holder, and it's very special to watch my friend and client play on Sundays. I also want to thank the forty or more Rams players and staff who allow me to work for them!

I want to also thank my friend Jared Goff. Being referred to Jared by his agent, Ryan Tollner, was a game changer. Meeting the number one pick of the 2016 NFL Draft and representing him in numerous deals has led to an awesome friendship. Thank you, Jared. Your loyalty and friendship are appreciated more than you can imagine.

I also want to thank all the business managers and sports agents who continue to refer clients my way. I've been fortunate to represent nearly 150 professional athletes through the years. I get a lot of them referred from player to player, but the majority come from agents and business managers. They are the golden geese for us real estate agents, and I worked hard to develop these lasting relationships. I'm grateful for them all.

A big thanks to Reggie and Lilit Bush. Whether it's a home in the Hollywood Hills, Pacific Palisades, or the San Fernando Valley, their loyalty is unmatched! They are amazing to work for, and I am incredibly grateful to call them friends.

Jacques McClendon—at the time of writing this book, Jacques is the director of football affairs for the LA Rams, and the Rams are lucky to have him. Jacques is a special guy. Personality plus, incredibly smart, MBA graduate from Brown University, and an incredible family man. He is also extremely important to my business. When the Rams moved from St. Louis to Los Angeles, every realtor in LA was fighting to develop a relationship with the team . . . most importantly, with Jacques. I'm the lucky one! Thanks, my friend.

I can't talk about athletes without thanking Don MacLean. Don is a retired NBA player, analyst, and also UCLA's all-time scorer. He was also my very first pro athlete. I was referred to him after he signed with the 76ers, by Dana and David Pump. Doing a great job for Don led to an introduction to his agent at the time, Arn Tellem. That was an introduction that I was going to take advantage of. That led to a dozen referrals, including my biggest game changer, Kobe Bryant!

I would be completely lost if it were not for my assistants, Kristi Dougherty and Madison Adams. Saying I would be lost without them is an understatement. As I mention in the book, I have severe ADD. In other words, I'm all over the place. I am also computer and technology illiterate, and if it were not for the patience and skills of these two, I would be lost. I have to also point out that Kristi has worked with me for seventeen years. I owe her the world! Thank you both for your hard work, dedication, and friendship.

I also want to thank all the other people I work with every day who help me transact my deals. I'm incredibly grateful for the following people.

Michael Kendrick and Victor Krotov with Landmark Escrow. For those of us in the business, we all depend on our escrow officers, and Michael and Victor are the best!

Ben Acosta and Jamie Angel—Fidelity National Title. They are the best in the business. I know I can always count on Ben and Jamie and Fidelity Title to get the job done.

I want to deeply thank my broker, Keith Myers. As independent contractors, productive agents can work wherever we want. In fact, we are all unrestricted free agents and can seek better "deals" from other brokerages in town. I'm here to say if it's not broke, don't fix it! I love Keith and all the support he gives me. Thanks for everything, Keith! You are an incredible broker and friend. I'm lucky I work for you!

RE/MAX—there is nowhere else I'd rather be. I love the people, the support, the leadership, and most of all the freedom to do what's best for my clients. I appreciate how RE/MAX allows us and supports us to build our own individual brands and teams (if desired), under a massive umbrella that is well respected all over the globe in more than a hundred countries. It's an honor to call RE/MAX my real estate family. Starting with the very top, the CEO Nick Bailey, and throughout the highest corporate levels of RE/MAX, I and the rest of the more than 140,000 agents can always count on the highest level of support.

To all my inspectors of choice. Each one of you is critical to my business, and I'm grateful for your skills, intelligence, and work ethic.

Jack Gironda—general inspector

Kevin Riley—Environmental Testing Associates, mold inspections

Kevin Stevenson—Ridamite, termite inspections

Michael Gerace—plumbing and sewer line

Billy Ridge—Conejo Valley Electric, the best electrician in Southern California

Joe Lavin—general inspector

I also want to thank my insurance agent Casey Clausen. Casey is not only an expert at home owners insurance but one of my best friends. I always know, when I refer a client to Casey, my clients will be extremely well taken care of for all their insurance needs.

On a personal note, I want to thank my dear friend Sophie Idan, owner of Sophisticate Interiors. Sophie is my number one home designer of choice. When given the opportunity, I always refer my clients to Sophie. She is truly an expert in home design.

And many more . . . thank you!

Special thanks to my dear friends and clients Bret and Kristi Michaels. Bret is not only an icon of rock and roll but also an author. When I told Bret about this book, he offered up some great advice that I incorporated. Thanks, Bret, love you, bro! I am also grateful that you graciously allowed me to tell the story of how we met and formed our business relationship and, more importantly, friendship. Thanks again, my brother.

For all of us real estate agents, we know it usually takes two to tango. In other words, we rely on one another to sell our listings and do deals. I'm lucky to have so many friends in our business who I am fortunate to work with every day. Sure we compete for listings, but it's always friendly, and fortunately there is enough business for all of us to be successful.

Big thanks to team Nicki LaPorta and Karen Crystal, Team Sigi and Pam, Marc Shevin, Mark Tyoran, and all the rest. I'm proud to say I love all of my colleagues whom I work with every day and appreciate you all!

Big thanks to my boys Josh and Matt Altman. Not only are the Altman Brothers incredibly successful and highly skilled, but they are two of my best friends in the game. I have been fortunate to have closed many deals with the Altman Brothers, and they are as good as advertised.

I want to also thank my Instagram mentors and friends that not only blow up my listings but have taught me so much along the way. Big thanks to Kambiz and Sina with @luxury_listings. Also want to thank @houses and all the other incredible pages and accounts that help me promote every day.

Huge thanks to Eric Simon and Matt Lionetti with Broke Agent Media. I'm incredibly grateful you agreed to participate in this book. Thank you for sharing your wisdom, knowledge, and experience in the social media game!

Taylor & Taylor—My friendship with Taylor Lautner started from an introduction from Thomas Tull and has continued for many years. Taylor purchased not only his first home with me but also several others. Truly one of the nicest big name celebs I've had the honor to represent. At the time of writing this book he is newly married to his beautiful wife who shares the same first name, Taylor. I want to wish them a lifetime of happiness.

Big thanks to the video teams I use. Thank you, Interior Pixels and Rial Productions! Grateful to have the best on my side!

Thank you to my photographer extraordinaire, Jeff Elson. I met Jeff more than fifteen years ago and have had the absolute pleasure to work with him ever since. Jeff is not only extremely skilled but one of the nicest guys I've ever met. He knows the exact angles and style that I love. I wrote an entire chapter on photography, and it's all because of Jeff Elson. Thank you, Jeff, for not only your friendship but for making me and my listings look their best.

Who gave me my start? That is none other than Todd Olson. Todd was the first broker I worked for, and he guided me through my first twenty years in the business. When I made the decision to give up my established business in the San Fernando Valley and literally move to a new county and start all over, Todd supported me. He opened a tiny office for me, and together we established ourselves in a new market from scratch. When he asked me if I would stick with him if he switched to RE/MAX, that was the easiest decision of my life. Thank you, Todd and the Olson family, for all your support, guidance, and friendship!

I cannot write a book without mentioning my best friends in the world, Paul and Caroline Jordan. Did they help me with business? No, but my life would not be the same without them. Paul has been like a true brother to me for forty-five years. Love you, guys.

I want to also thank my dear friends Frank and Julie Kashare. Frank owns the mega motocross company O'Neal. Frank is also one of the smartest people I know, and he helped through this book-writing journey. Thanks for all your advice, Frankie!

I also want to thank my dear friend Brent Polacheck. Brent is one of the most generous guys I know. Brent and Polacheck's Jewelers have not only become dear friends but also enable me to satisfy my addiction to fine watches.

I also want to thank our friends Steve and Christine Goldstein. Love you, guys! I literally talk to Steve every day. He is one of the best and most loyal friends anyone can ever ask for.

Words cannot express my gratitude for two of my oldest and dearest friends, Dana and David Pump. The Pump Brothers and I grew up together, and they introduced me to the sports community, which changed my life. Thanks, boys, for everything.

Speaking of brothers . . . I want to thank mine. My big brother, Al Cohen. Al taught me right from wrong growing up and always looked after me. I love you, bro . . . and your wonderful wife, my sister-in-law, Connie, and my niece, McKenna.

Keeping with family, just a dedication is not enough for my parents, Arnie and Harriet Cohen. At the time of this book my dad is ninety and my mom is eighty-six. Nobody has had a bigger impact on my life than they have. I could not say enough about my parents. Love them more than anything and am grateful for all they have done for me. I love ya, Ma. I love ya, Pops. Thanks for being the best parents anyone could ever dream of!

As with my parents, when speaking about my beautiful wife, Becky, and my kids, Cameron and Cassidy, a simple book dedication is not enough. I've been married to my amazing wife for thirty years, and I owe her everything. The obvious is the unconditional love and constant support, but you don't want to read about that. It's what she did for my business that is astounding. Not only did she hand deliver my first listing, her parent's home, but she role-played with me every night for more than six months to help me hone my skills. She has allowed me to give up too many weekends to count, put up with my twenty-four-hour-a-day cell phone habits, and has always been there for me through every shitty escrow. Thanks, Babe. Everything we got is because of you, and I love you more than life.

To my amazing kids, Cameron and Cassidy, thank you. I tried to be home as often as I could, but I'm sure there were many disappointing weekends where mom had to say, "I'm sorry, but Dad has to work." I love you both so very much and appreciate you more than you will ever know. I am proud of the responsible adults you have both grown to be.

Lastly, thank you to you, the reader, who actually took the time to read this far. I am so incredibly grateful for you.